International Textbooks
in Art and Art Education

Italo L. de Francesco
Consulting Editor

Orientation to Drawing and Painting

Orientation to Drawing and Painting

Robert Henkes

Kalamazoo Public Schools
and
Kalamazoo Institute of Arts
Kalamazoo, Michigan

International Textbook Company
Scranton, Pennsylvania

PREFACE

This book is not a step-by-step procedure of drawing and painting activities; rather, it is a book dealing with art experiences presented in a direct approach. The drawing and painting experiences discussed are direct in nature and are designed to erase incompetence and frustration and bring about self-discipline and confidence.

Each chapter deals with a specific type of drawing or painting experience, and each experience has a specific purpose. The art teacher must know in what capacity each approach must be used and to what extent. Furthermore, the table of contents need not dictate the order of procedure. The teacher may use any chapter as the need for it arises. For example, I believe that contour drawing should be presented in the first weeks of school, but others may decide that a painting experience is more suitable for that time.

Finally, this book does not indicate a specific time element. The art experiences suggested could cover the entire year, depending on class size, ability, and differences. I have attempted to present the major types or approaches to drawing and painting and the purposes involved in each.

ROBERT HENKES

Kalamazoo, Michigan
January, 1965

ACKNOWLEDGMENTS

The author's thanks are here expressed to the students of the Kalamazoo Public Schools and the Kalamazoo Institute of Arts whose works are reproduced in this book. Thanks also go to Marion Andros, Supervisor of Art; Dr. Richard N. Percy, Superintendent of Schools, and Mr. Alfred Maurice, Director of the Institute of Arts, Kalamazoo, Michigan.

Further thanks go to *School Arts* magazine, edited by Dr. John W. Cataldo and Elizabeth Cataldo, and to *Arts and Activities* magazine, edited by Dr. F. Louis Hoover and Betty Lou Munson, for permission to utilize material from articles by the author which appeared in those publications.

Further thanks must go to Kenneth R. Gromlich and John A. Wargo for their advice and patience in the final preparations of this book.

ROBERT HENKES

TABLE OF CONTENTS

LIST OF ILLUSTRATIONS

MODES OF ART   1

Any orientation to drawing and painting as art expressions should include an appreciation of the drawing and painting done by great artists and the understanding that great artists have expressed themselves in a number of different modes. This emphasizes the individual approach inherent in all artistic expressions, and the necessity to retain one's personality as it is transmitted from nature to the canvas.

Frequently, the student will express an idea contrary to his personality; that is, the technique used will be alien to his potential self because of an unawareness that other techniques exist. As the student proceeds through the various schools of painting, he may uncover a more adjustable means of self-expression. Furthermore, he may realize the relationship of his newly found approach to that of artists of centuries before in their attempts to discover more personal means of expression. A greater appreciation of the painter, his expression, and the time in which he lived will then be enjoyed by the student.

The project in art appreciation relating to the modes or styles of art proposed in this chapter may be considered for use in an actual art class or in a class concerned with the study of the history of art. Each would have a different set of purposes and points of evaluation. The project would entail the study of different periods or schools of painting by active engagement in the process of painting. If introduced in the art class, focal attention to the techniques and procedures must be established to foster an individual relationship between technique and personality.

The introduction of this project to an academic class will be similar to that to an art class, but certain qualifications must be made because the student is not necessarily interested in art as a creative experience. Consequently, newly obtained knowledge should be evaluated academically, with the experience of painting deepening that knowledge and clarifying the position of the painter. The purpose of the project will be the furtherance of knowledge through explorational research—the study of different techniques and the application of paint to paper in

Naturalism. This is an attempt at naturalistic expression; it portrays detail visually comprehensible to the student.

2

Impressionism. This is an attempt at impressionistic painting; the colors were placed side by side, depending upon the vision to suggest the blending of colors.

order to duplicate these techniques. By these means, the student will somewhat realize the problems involved in particular styles of painting and willingly accept the painter in a more appreciative manner. The techniques, or schools of painting, to be discussed and demonstrated in the illustrations in this chapter are Naturalism, Impressionism, Cubism, Abstractionism, Expressionism, and Surrealism. Other schools may be used, depending on the background, personality, attitudes, and ability of the teacher. The selection may also depend on the temperament, size, and ability of the class. The six schools of painting just mentioned have been selected because each serves a different need and because they have been proved the most successful over the years. Students should illustrate the technique of each of the six schools in the form of a painting.

The initial move, the selection of a motivating force, is most important. The motivating force for the first painting (Naturalism) may be 1) a photograph of nature from a magazine or newspaper, 2) an actual photograph taken by the student, or 3) an actual on-the-spot drawing of nature. Each of these approaches is valid, because it is not the source, but the result of the motivation that counts. The selection of a photograph from a periodical enables those students who lack ideas to choose from a wide range of stimuli. Those who desire to combine photography with art may set the stage for the six paintings by composing their own setting or settings. Herein lies a practical creative experience in itself; for photography can be an invigorating and dramatic creative form. The groundwork can be set by discussions of composition: unusual angle shots, detail concentration, rare subject matter, and double exposures.

The third approach is generally taken by those students who are competent in drawing, who draw naturally and with ease any subject matter placed before them. Before beginning his painting, the student must determine one other course: whether to allow the first painting to dictate the composition of the other five, or whether each succeeding painting will be of a different subject and thus cause a complete change in composition.

Let us consider the first course. From the original selection, photograph, or drawing the student now proceeds to paint in exact detail the color, composition, contrast, and mood evidenced in his original stimulus. The first painting may be of any size, but once that is established, the dimensions of the remaining five paintings must be identical

4

with those of the first. This uniformity demands discipline in the placement of subject matter within limits. The student needs boundaries within which to work; he must adjust the subject matter to the working surface, never the working surface to the subject matter. Also, this uniformity of size presents the student with a sense of order. But more important is its relation to the transition of the original ideas to the succeeding five paintings.

Since the first painting (Naturalism) is an attempt to copy or duplicate the original photograph or drawing in an effort to strengthen concentration and observation, its complexity will necessarily exceed that of the paintings in the five remaining techniques of painting.

The second painting (Impressionism) must incorporate all compositional elements present in the Naturalistic painting but be executed in the Impressionist method. This may involve the application of dots, dashes, streaks, or blotches of color. It would be wise to use only one of these methods in order to minimize confusion in the mind of the student and to compel a consistency in the expression. Constant referral to the initial painting (Naturalism) is necessary, since it acts as the stimulus for future production.

In applying color impressionistically the student mixes the color directly on the paper by placing different colors side by side or by slightly overlapping them. In this way an actual mixing of color with the brush does not take place. The problem of the apparent isolation of color is solved by the distance or space between the viewer and the painting: the eye acts as the agent by which the color is formed.

The colors used in this mixing method must be identical with those in the first painting (Naturalism) and identified by similar placement. For example, if the initial painting is a landscape in which a tree is expressed and if that tree is painted brown, that same tree, identifiable in the Impressionistic painting by its placement, must also be painted brown. That is, its existence will be expressed by placing relatively close to each other those colors that constitute the color brown, namely, red, yellow, and blue. This procedure is followed throughout the painting. Of course, as the process continues, it is also necessary to solve the problems of contrast, shading, and creating three-dimensional qualities.

Aside from the appreciation value, two major factors of learning result directly from this method of painting: 1) the knowledge of color and 2) the knowledge of mixing color to form recessive areas. In learn-

Cubism. Cubism is evident here in the background, as well as in the natural object, the tree.

6

Abstractionism. Overlapping planes interpenetrate in shape and color in this abstract version of the same subject; the background comes forward and the foreground recedes.

7

ing color, the student is frequently faced with the problem of constituting a color, as, for example, placing the colors red and yellow adjacent to each other to form the color orange. Even though the colors are isolated, the eye transforms them into a single color.

The blending of color to form recessive areas is particularly useful in depicting the facial features of the human form. It is difficult to portray the nose and surrounding areas in their respective tones, and the Impressionistic method lessens the frustration by applying the proper colors side by side. An area such as the nose is lightened by placing more dots or streaks of white; an area is darkened by using darker colors in the same manner. This approach to painting frequently encourages the student to express subject matter previously considered beyond his ability.

In expressing the third school of painting (Cubism), the student must again refer to the initial painting. The cube has been considered by artists as the basis of form. Cubistically expressing an idea demands concentration on both the objects and the space surrounding them. Here again the student must depict the objects in the first painting in their approximate size and placement. Each object must then be developed into a cube, after which attention is directed to cubing the space. This may become a complex problem, because each object suggests numerous potential cubes in the space surrounding it. Therefore, the student must be careful not to allow the space to dominate the theme.

After the student has completed the drawing, color is applied to the cubed sections. Since the cube generally has three visible sides, each side will be a shade or tone of a single color. A tree, for example, would be painted light brown, dark brown, and brown to define the three sections of the cube. This procedure is used for all the areas painted.

Besides its outlined purpose, cubistic painting points up the importance of three-dimensional form on a two-dimensional surface. It also promotes growth in the process of darkening and lightening colors.

Abstractionism, the fourth school of painting listed, will perhaps be least understood by the student. Abstractionism is often considered "any art expression which is nonunderstandable and nonrecognizable," "a design without meaning," "chaos, confusion, and disorganization," "a conglomeration of lines, dots, blotches, and smears executed without thought," or "anything that has nothing to do with art." These state-

8

ments are typical of student reaction to abstract art. The greatest barrier to accepting Abstractionism is misinterpretation; so appreciation is indeed long overdue.

In depicting the initial ideas in abstract form, the student should be cautioned not to confuse this form with that of Cubism. The overlap can be avoided by the insistence of flatly painted areas, which can be accomplished simply by the method of interpenetration (bringing the outside in and the inside out). For example, if the initial drawing (Naturalism) depicts two trees standing in front of a house, an abstract quality is immediately evidenced by extending the lines of the house through or in front of the trees. When an object overlaps another object, the object that is farther back in the picture plane is partially covered, with the result that if the front object were removed, in this case the trees, the entire house would be visible. Thus, the purpose of Abstractionism is to view two or more objects at the same time by overlapping and interpenetrating them.

In order for Abstractionism to retain its form during the process of painting, it is necessary that there be a close relationship between the colors of the overlapped objects. Using the same situation of the house and trees, one may veer farther from reality. For example, if the color of the house is red and the tree is painted white, then that part of the tree overlapping the house will be expressed in pink. The retention of form demands this type of color adjustment. If the entire tree were painted white, interpenetration would not exist, nor would the abstraction.

Overlapped segments of the painting, then, should be depicted in the combination of the colors caused by the two overlapping objects. The introduction of an intense color in an overlapped area would destroy the order of the painting, and it is this maintenance of order that puzzles the student. If the painting suddenly begins to "fall apart," it is generally due to an improper color occupying an overlapped area. One of the major appreciative factors resulting from this method of painting is the expression of numerous objects or ideas in a single area.

Expressionism, the fifth school of painting, is perhaps the most difficult to comprehend, partly because of the difficulty in communicating to the student the idea of emotion. Expressionism is an intuitive blast of emotion that takes form on canvas or paper and is executed in a comparatively brief period of time. Its apparent uncontrollability arises

9

Expressionism. Here color is not defined as contrast but rather is blended during the process of the intuitive act of painting.

10

Surrealism. This surrealistic attempt to depict the same composition reveals the cloud as a fish and the tree as strong spiral buildings.

from an intense struggle of restraint and drive. It is like a tug-of-war in which two opposing forces are attempting to win. Because the two are of equal force, the tension remains activated throughout the struggle. The struggle of the Expressionist painter lies in the strong urge to sprawl his emotions onto canvas and simultaneously control them.

This is indeed a difficult task for the student, for he seldom relates an emotional release to the experience of painting, especially abstract painting. The visual world is his major concern.

But here the task of the student is simplified, because the initial painting acts as a starting point. The student should strengthen the visual and emotional response of the Naturalistic painting in order that the point of departure to the Expressionistic painting is at a high pitch. Then he should paint his emotional reaction to the original painting in a continuous span of time. Once he has exhausted his emotional energy in what he considers a complete expression, he no longer is concerned with it. However, he may repeat the process by doing successive paint-tings until personal satisfaction results.

The subject matter of the original expression may dictate an emotional response in varying degree. If the Naturalistic painting presents an obvious quality of emotion such as delicacy, charm, stillness, drama, or excitement, the Expressionistic portrayal of that emotion may result quite simply by using soft, subtle colors representing delicacy and charm in a caressing and softening touch of the brush, whereas drama and excitement may be reflected with slashing strokes of the brush. So the goal of the Expressionists is to satisfy an intuitive urge to express an emotional reaction to nature.

The final painting, and the one from which the student will receive the most enjoyment, is Surrealistic. Again reference is made to the original composition for identical placement of objects. The student now changes the objects present in the first painting to objects of unreality. Trees may change to pencils or paint brushes; rocks may become minute unmbrellas; an automobile can take the form of an animal, with oversized claws acting as the wheels, a tail substituted for the exhaust pipe, a neck replacing the hood, and eyes replacing the headlights. This may all appear ridiculous, but further investigation will reveal some individual characteristics previously untapped.

Surrealism is a form or approach to art that considers the subconscious imagination as the real and the conventions and laws by which we are governed as the unreal. Of course, the surrealist artist shuns conventional society, but the student is not equipped or permitted to act in that fashion. However, because the whimsical is allowed to take over this final painting in the name of Surrealism, the student does express inner feelings in concrete form without realizing it. His choice of substituted subject matter may reflect individual personality and character. Furthermore, a consistent similarity in changes indicates a complete idea. Dissimilarity of change or inconsistency of similarity indicates a disassociation of ideas.

The actual purpose involved here is to completely transform the original idea of the Naturalistic painting to one of unreality or fantasy. The Surrealist painting, too, must be a complete expression; that is, uniformity must exist within each form or object as well as the whole. The idea of this painting must be completely detached, except for identical placement of each of the objects, so that upon its completion there is no similarity to the initial painting except in compositon.

A second course which might be followed, if desired, was mentioned earlier, that each of the six paintings may stem from a different stimulus or idea. In other words, each painting can be different in size, in subject matter, and in composition. In this manner, the student need not follow the pattern of the first painting, but can initiate a new idea with each painting. This would not be advisable except in instances in which the student may be hampered in his creative growth. It would permit more freedom, but it would also demand a greater degree of control.

This study in the "Modes of Art" has been presented in the hope that more individuals might learn by doing the painting, and by technical realization might more deeply understand the techniques used by the artist and the purposes that these techniques serve.

Since many student drawings and paintings reveal stereotype ideas, techniques, compositions, and color selection, the stage is now set for direct approaches to graphic expression and the use of natural stimuli. Above all, the painting assignments in this chapter are studies in self-discipline which constitute a direction toward the elimination of stereotype symbols. It also promotes reflective thinking and rigidity in compositional order essential to all art forms.

Since this opening chapter is a study in self-discipline, its need is further amplified in the following chapter indicating diverse attitudes in educational theory which propagate the extremes in art education.

SUGGESTED ACTIVITIES

1. Study the schools or periods of painting of past history to the present.

2. Study the changes of the twentieth century in art.

3. Study the development of a single painter (Picasso, Greene, Guston, Rouault, Miro).

4. Collect, sketch, or photograph examples of art in nature that resembles abstract design.

5. Study paintings of the Surrealists.

6. Practice painting quick—one- to five-minute—sketches of a posed model.

7. Meditate for ten minutes; then in five minute's time execute a painting.

8. Study carefully the composition of an abstract painting.

9. Paint a single figure expressing two different emotions or personalities.

10. Paint a series of cubes and show the inside and outside of each cube without the use of outlines.

ORIENTATION TO DRAWING   2

Techniques vary in determining courses of study. Some educators believe that freedom of expression can best be served by immediately detaching students from fears of insecurities. For example, inability to draw is removed by the introduction and execution of activities that do not involve the problems of expressing the visual in natural terms, or if they do, that are carried out in a style that discourages visual perception. This inevitably leads to abstractions, and the understanding of oneself is directed through abstract symbols. This is unfair to the students, because they never master the most essential element of nature and of art: that of overcoming insecurities through a most natural means.

Drawing and painting must be natural; but in order for one to express freely the stimulus of nature, one must first become the master of nature. Otherwise, slavery will exist and continue to monopolize the student until a thorough attempt is made to overcome insecurities by the proper means. Freedom exists only after the student has control over both the ideas he wishes to express and the manner in which they are expressed.

One of the major considerations to be noted is the lack of subjective approaches. Objectivity is overwhelmingly present; and if art is to materialize, the personality of the expressor as well as the expression must come into existence. Otherwise, the student is not yet involved with his idea. He still exists outside the realm of experience. He must enter into the experience subjectively so that the outside does not exist. Objective representation of nature is not unusual. It is normal in an objective world, but art is subjective. It is highly personal. It is oneself, expressed to the satisfaction of oneself.

The student is generally nonreflective, and consequently visual representation is evident. He must draw what he sees, as he sees it; and only strong emotional reactions will cause a change in approach and ultimately a change in expression. If reflective meditation is not demanded of the student, numerous incidentals seep into the expression because no direct course has been set.

The idea must be strengthened as the expression develops. If the idea is not fully expressed, there will be evidence of objectivity. Ideas alien to the initial purpose, although legitimate under certain circumstances, will destroy the original concept; that is, succeeding ideas could destroy the original concept and cause a change in the entire expression. For example, an automobile accident may be the initial step toward an understanding and realization of the tremendous loss to humanity. Yet, placing hope, in the form of medical care, in a remote area of the expressed depiction may cause the student to reverse the importance of the two ideas. One is beneficial to the other, and the importance attached to each depends upon the subjective reactions toward the two.

The student may now realize that to place emphasis upon hope rather than tragedy is to have a more humanitarian and charitable outlook. And so the expression begins to change. Only when an idea completely absorbs the student will such a change transpire. Identical ideas may exist in another expression with no particular significance. That is why the attempt toward a completely objective portrayal of nature needs to be sidelined, perhaps permanently, so that art expression truly becomes a release from mental, physical, and spiritual confusions.

Incidentals are also evident in thoughts that are unexpressed in objective fashion and difficult to ascertain. These will be expressed in the wavering of a line, in the thickness or darkness of a line, and in the sudden angle or direction of a line. For example, figure drawing is one form of expression in which this type of uncertainty is evident. The student reveals insecurities in two different ways: by unconsciously changing the tempo of his drawing through daydreaming and by consciously changing his expression because of his inability to draw visually what is before him.

Daydreaming is more pertinent to incidental wavering because it is done unconsciously. Furthermore, it is caused by a lack of interest at the precise time that the drawing is taking place. This lack of interest is not necessarily the fault of the teacher, since the thoughts occupying the mind of the student are more important than the activity at hand. As the drawing progresses, the eye and mind collaborate. Suddenly, or

16

gradually, alien thoughts cause the progression, intensity, or character of the line to change, contrary to the visual representation of the figures. The more frequent these intrusions, the more likely the student is to give up.

It would be highly beneficial if these interruptions could be channeled into respected forms of expression. This could come about by resolving the real problem: the cause of the interruption. Or the art experience could be so demanding or inspiring as to overshadow, at least temporarily, the real problem.

More prevalent is the occurrence of conscious incidentals. Frustration exists because the student is aware of his incompetence. Yet, in such cases, proper direction can be projected almost immediately.

The student will balk when drawing facial features, and frequently a strongly inserted incidental line will obliterate an area difficult to express. This line acts as a shield. In another instance, the student will add lines to an area as a "fill in" method and thus excuse himself from solving the problem. Still another student will resort to suggestion, thereby not completing the expression of the object and priding himself on being clever. And there are those who completely omit particular features because they frankly admit their inadequacy to depict them.

In order to overcome such practicing falsehoods, the student must no longer rely on imaginative symbols that take the form of stereotypes. It should suffice to mention only a few. Predominately evident are historical characterizations; trees that take on the shapes of lollipops and icecream cones; mountains that are perfectly and meticulously rounded out; formally balanced compositions equally distant at all sides; facial features involving turned-up noses, watermelon mouths, and elongated eyelashes; homes that appear more suitable for dolls than human beings; and modes of transportation that date back to the nineteenth century.

One must be extremely careful not to confuse stereotype symbols with expressed characteristics. One of the major differences is that a characteristic is an artistic symbol typical of a student at a particular stage of growth, whereas a stereotype is an imaginative symbol that is generally devoid of visual and factual knowledge and that relates to an earlier age. A characteristic is true to nature in an individual and personalized way. It is distortion based on a sound knowledge of nature at a particular stage of mental growth.

Both the stereotype and the characteristic originate in early childhood. The vast difference lies in the source from which each develops—the stereotype from imagination and memory; the characteristic from method and habit. The stereotype reveals a stunted growth imaginatively, emotionally, and intellectually, whereas the possibilities of development are potentially strong in the case of the characteristic.

Those who exhibit a repeated stereotype pattern of growth will find it difficult to expand emotional freedom, because both the visual and factual capacities have been deeply damaged. However, there always remain possibilities so long as the teacher and the student have patience to nurture the prevailing interest. In such cases, one must tend toward the emotional ladder, since color is a factor in painting that can be uncovered and propagated to a high degree. Because the stereotype is based on imagination and memory, it is legitimate in the earlier stages of growth, but repeated performances during succeeding years only reveal a stagnancy difficult to overcome. This is due to the interest in art being sidelined or to the low intellectual capacity of the student.

Such stereotypes as reversions to historical characterization generally reflect an interest in different types of historical literature, but it is still an excuse not to venture into the twentieth century. It is also a source of security, since undoubtedly success came this way previously, either in a misguided art unit or in a social studies class.

Formally balanced compositions may not appear as stereotypes, but they are unquestionably barriers to creative growth. Regardless of the multiplicity or originality of ideas, the arrangement can be as stagnant as the ideas themselves. Nothing is more sterile than a focal point of interest flanked by objects identical in size, shape, and color. It would be wise to discourage such prearranged mental setups and encourage off-balanced compositions as the initial move. They can be encouraged quite readily by establishing activities that demand visual comprehension. When the student relies on memory for an idea to be expressed,

18

he can only envision the idea as he would like it to be. Dictation through visual necessity is possible only if he uses nature as a stimulus.

Defining student characteristics in relation to graphic expression is more difficult in that the expression is a true one, even though distortion is much in evidence. It is the distortion that is confused with stereotype. Stereotype is not nature; it is a childish image of nature. This excludes, of course, formalized compositions that deal with the arrangement of things. The things to be composed can surely be natural, but the manner of placement is an often repeated pattern resulting in sterility.

The expression of the human figure repeatedly relates misproportions. But these miscalculations are basically correct and their presence has psychological importance. For example, the large head related to tiny hands is often due to the extreme significance attached to the head. This in an emotional reaction toward others in that the face of the individual is far more important than his hands. Because the hands are expressed rather modestly does not indicate an incorrect drawing. The hands may be basically sound in construction; but by their diminutive size in relation to the head, the student expresses their relative significance.

Most important is the fact that a characteristic may develop as the student develops. Characteristics such as the outlining of objects, flat application of color, exaggerated proportions, lack of perspective, and even tactual and visual representation in a single composition will take on charm, strength, drama, and refinement if the student is encouraged to continue along characteristic lines of his age group.

The outline is a legitimate technique if it is used to accent or strengthen an idea. The outline is a growth from earlier years when the child outlined his idea, and upon completion, filled in the outlined drawing with color. As the child matures, he realizes that the main ideas of his picture appear weak. Yet he does not generally know that poor contrast is the cause of the weakness. So in order to reinforce his idea, he surrounds it with an outline. And because of continued misuse of the outline, he fails to benefit fully from color relationships.

Exaggerated proportions, naturally expressed, generally reveal poetic qualities seldom found in picturizations that lean toward naturalistic portrayal. Characteristics are precious and should be preserved and developed individually as long as the student retains a high degree of interest and satisfaction. Such a student is as yet unspoiled by the realization of purely visual representation.

The visual refers to that which the eye sees. Thus, to be visually minded is merely the beginning; for without the heart and soul, the expression simply states what is seen. But the essence of art lies not only in what is expressed through sight but in what is experienced through the love, sympathy, understanding, hatred, or resentment that one feels toward another. In order to retain this essential quality of emotion, the student must choose the time at which, the manner in which, and the degree to which he wishes to be affected. The characteristics briefly described may undergo a change, but one must attempt to retain the essential character of the individual expression and parallel it with both intellectual and emotional stimuli.

The types of artistic experiences described in the following chapters are attempts to maintain individuality while developing both the visual and the emotional qualities simultaneously.

CONTOUR DRAWING **3**

The preceding chapter strongly indicates the need for a direct approach to drawing. The illustrations that accompany the chapter on orientation reveal uncertainties between the student's knowledge of nature, his visual perception of nature, his emotional reaction toward nature, and his eventual expression of nature.

If the student has reached a stage of indifference toward drawing because of pride or inability to master natural forms, it seems necessary to sharpen his visual perception in order to elude the danger of objective repetition. This development of visual awareness is the initial purpose of contour drawing, which is frequently misinterpreted as outline drawing. Drawing in contour is conceived and executed in a three-dimensional nature because of the concentrated effort it demands in depicting three-dimensional form.

The student directs his eyes upon the object being portrayed and draws while his eyes are focused on the object. Motivation of this type of drawing depends largely upon the individual teacher, and an atmosphere of sincerity, honesty, and seriousness should prevail before contour drawing can fulfill its purpose. The teacher must explain that a concentrated effort is essential and that mistakes will be made, but that these mistakes must be accepted and overcome. Students will attempt to erase lines or include extra lines in order to rectify mistakes. This reaction is normal, but it must be discouraged.

Let us step into an art classroom in which a student has volunteered to model. The teacher explains: "Focus your eyes on a particular spot on the model. Now place your pencil on an appropriate place on your paper. Look, and draw. As your eye follows the shape of the head, your pencil should do likewise." The teacher further explains: "Keep your eyes on the model. Do not look at your paper, even though it is a great temptation. When your eye and hand have completely followed the contour of the model, and have reached the starting point, then look at your paper." At this moment there will be laughter, discouragement,

GUNTIS MIKELSONS

Single figures (set of three). Here the emphasis is on the position and personality of the posed model; contour lines reveal an intense concentration on types of poses.

22

and perhaps even resentment. It is at this time that the teacher reinforces the seriousness of this form of expression by establishing a sound attitude throughout the class. Emphasis is placed upon the belief that a true expression depends not on accurately duplicating the model, but on individuality. Each student's drawing should be displayed from an affirmative viewpoint, either through classroom procedure or personal contacts.

The student soon realizes his true difficulties and his particular problems; and with reassurance and a renewed effort, he begins to regard himself as an individual, uniquely different from his classmates. He begins to realize that even though he is considered a well coordinated person in other aspects, he lacks the capability of keen observation. Once this capability of careful observation is acquired by the student, attention is directed to the relationship of visual perception to emotional response. The eye serves only as a means of conveying emotion, but the eye must observe discriminately the object being expressed.

Emotion, in itself, must be controlled, and the eye is a factor in this control. Distortion stems only from a full knowledge of the object, and subsequently the two—knowledge and distortion—become synonymous. So it is with contour drawing. The eye acts first and emotion controls the discriminating eye. Subsequently, also, the actual seeing of the object and the emotion involved in expressing that object become one and the same.

In developing a keener observation of nature through sight, one is enabled to erase concepts that are no longer imaginative and that are obstacles to future use and development. The student must observe nature as he is drawing so that the eye and any emotion connected with the object are working together. This is necessary, and it is not easily done. We are concerned with the technique of contour drawing only to the extent that it enables one to accentuate the positive aspects of nature. It is a form of concentration on a given object of nature. It leaves no room for uncertainties, and it is concerned solely with the feeling one possesses for the object portrayed. It initiates a challenge for those prone to succumb to conventionalism.

This type of drawing reaps the greatest rewards for those who become strictly objective and lean toward a style of drawing. The word "style" must be distinguished from the subjective approach. There are those who draw subjectively and there are those who draw objec-

EVA DUBBELD

LINDA BLISS

LINDA BLISS

TERRY STEVENS

JUNIOR ESTES

Faces (set of three). The concentration of these facial features reveals the personality of the model, as well as that of the artist.

24

AT THE ZOO. *Here single and group poses challenged the student to compose an idea on a given working surface. The background was added to coincide with the position of the models.*

25

IN THE SCHOOLROOM. *Although the models differed in personality, the personality of the artist is evident throughout this complete contour drawing.*

WAITING IN THE LIBRARY. *The group positioning of these figures is consistent throughout the composition; the line background produces the idea.*

tively. Subjectivity reflects personality, one's own personal approach, and this reflection is unconscious. "Style," in this instance, refers to those who consciously depict all things in the same objective manner. The student reveals no personality in the objects portrayed, or in his own makeup. To succumb to such a style stunts the student's creative and intellectual growth, because he has reached a plateau and remains there until his interest in art is lost.

Evaluation

To evaluate any art form is a difficult matter. Contour drawing must be judged by the exactitude of eye and hand coordination in relation to the complexity of the expression. Emotional quality must then be considered as a final determinant. This quality of emotion is an elusive thing that can be judged according to the visual stimulus, namely, the posed model; or it can be evaluated according to distortions or exaggerations. One cannot be sure of the subconscious reaction the student may express in his drawing, and so the judgment becomes a precarious one. Yet, perhaps, not so precarious if the emotional quality tends to exaggerate bodily features or positions. For example, a tall slender model may be drawn in such a way as to accentuate the slenderness, or

27

Time for Recitation. *The lined background augments the idea for these well-established poses; textures and solidly-filled areas were added.*

an obtrusive facial feature may be expressed in an extremely unattractive manner. Because of the concentration demanded, seemingly exaggerated features will be made more distorted, and this, in turn, will reflect emotion.

One may stop here and evaluate the emotional character on this basis. However, since contour drawing is executed primarily to promote keener observational powers, it is not in the strictest contour sense, justified to evaluate on emotional content that reflects exaggerations; for after progressive and extensive practice, portrayal that is more exact proportionately will result. And so it seems that the judgment should be made purely on visual perception; that is, the more detailed and exacting the account of the stimulus, namely, the model, the more highly rated should be the drawing.

If, then, successive drawings reveal an almost exact duplication of the model, does one no longer consider the emotional quality? Regardless of the exactness of the portrayal, emotional character will exert itself because of its subjective nature. Bodily features may eventually be executed proportionately correct; but because of the extreme concentration demanded, emotion will exist within the proportionately correct drawing.

Complexity is also a determining factor in the judgment of contour drawing. A single figure or object is a simple matter; but with the addition of other objects or figures, one must consider the more complex process of overlapping and spacing.

Then, finally, one must evaluate those students who never reach the point of exactitude, that is, whose eye and hand coordination is not mastered. One may simply count the mistakes and evaluate accordingly. Some drawings may be highly incoherent; thus evaluation would be extremely low. A mistake may be considered to be a disconnected line or an overlapping line—a line that does not reach its point of contact or a line that overshoots the point of contact. Either indicates a lack of complete correlation. Incidentally, each line has a source from which it begins, so that lines that begin and end within a given shape and with no point of contact would be deemed mistakes.

Above all other criteria, the student as an individual must, of course, be evaluated on growth; for unquestionably students progress in varying degrees, and unless each expression is evaluated in relation to the respective student, art education falls short of its goal.

HOMEWORK. *This back view of a model presents an effective idea; textural variations improve the mere outline drawing.*

30

SUGGESTED ACTIVITIES

1. Set up a simple still life, and draw it with stress on variety of lines.

2. Draw a simple standing figure (posed by student) draped with simple clothing.

3. Select an object from the art room and draw its contour. Place a similar object next to it, and draw only the outside contour of the two as a single unit.

4. Select a group of students whose clothing varies in simplicity, texture, and type of material.

5. Select different physical structures of students to forward emotional expression.

6. Using a group of figures, draw a background view of the classroom, the outside of the school, or a hallway. Adapt the background to the figures.

7. Draw heads, hands, and feet as a daily exercise.

8. Suggest homework, such as the drawing of pets, family, dinner table, and kitchen.

9. Draw outdoor scenes of buildings; draw segments of the same buildings.

10. Draw hands, changing the position of the fingers after each drawing.

Single standing figure (2-minute sketch). This simple pose enabled the student to express the position quickly; both the tip and the side of the crayon were used.

32

GESTURE DRAWING   4

Gesture drawing has never been given the attention it deserves. In fact, too frequently, it has been misrepresented and misinterpreted. "To gesture" means to move into action. The common expression, "It is a good gesture to give to those who need it," is indeed a gesture of action. The actual physical presentation that is governed by mental, emotional, and intellectual attitudes is precisely the one seen in the gesture drawings that accompany this chapter.

It is necessary to realize that gesture drawing is not simply drawing a circular form in spirals or circular lines in an effort to establish a particular position or a positive action. It is the anticipation of a future act or an ensuing intuitive response to a previous act. The student must be able to do more than detect or see the physical position of the person being expressed. He must place himself in the same state of being as the model, in so far as that is possible. It is not easy and it does not become a reality except after much thought and experience. It demands sensitivity and a willingness to "wear oneself out." Relaxation is the key to successful gesture drawing, but the freedom to relax does not come until one releases oneself from the tenseness that initially accompanies gesture drawing.

Furthermore, gesture drawing is a combination and unification of all parts. If one reacts emotionally to a tragic scene, his whole being is affected. So with the model when imitating an emotional state, and so with the student expressing the same tragedy. It is essential that the cause of the gesture be drawn as the most significant force and that all other gestures contribute to the whole. Gesture does not refer only to action in the sense of movable parts; it may be as evident in the mute pose of a beggar seeking his alms as it is in the torturous, agonizing swirl of muscles in a heavyweight wrestling match.

The student is attempting to gain through gesture drawing a realization of the emotion involved in the pose of the model and its transference to himself with a resulting expression in graphic form. As contour

MAURICE HERN

Seated half figure. A free moving ballpoint pen enabled the student to express the subject quickly; this 30-second sketch reveals the student's confidence in expressing gesture.

drawing develops visual perception, gesture drawing develops emotional perception. Of course, contour drawing stimulates emotional perception, but its attainment is a result of the subconscious. That is, one does not objectively seek emotional traits of the person being portrayed in the course of contour drawing, but because of its concentrated nature, the emotion possessed releases itself unconsciously. This may also come about in gesture drawing, but the initial purpose is to seek objectively the gestured characteristics of the model but to express them subjectively.

34

EVA DUBBERD

Detailed seated figure. Here free-flowing lines indicate the relaxed position of the model; additional lines reflect the weight and personality of the model.

The question whether the gesture expressed by the student overplays its part is an important one. Exaggeration and distortion are certainly called for, but they must be expressed intuitively. They must be sensed rather than thought out. To think of a state of emotion while subjectively expressing it is impossible; that is, to deliberately distort means to objectively distort. This means, then, that a subjective reaction and a subjective expression cannot result. Subjectivity stems from the heart, not from the mind.

AT THE WHARF (group figures). Here a group pose was transformed into an idea for a future painting.

36

COMBO *(group figures). This is a gesture drawing of a practice session in the band room; the student positioned himself so that overlapping is evident in the group pose.*

Let us assume that subjective distortion takes place. It must then be noted that an exaggerated emotional reaction to the model does not eliminate or subordinate other gestures of the model. For example, the model may position himself in a cramped style indicating pain. Yet a glimmer of relief may be evidenced in the turn or tilt of the mouth. It is this combination of gestures that is difficult to express in the same drawing.

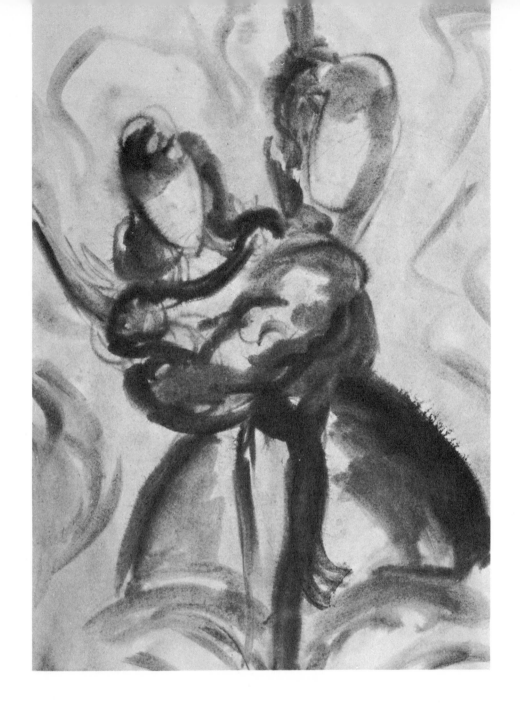

MOTHER AND CHILD. *Brush and ink on wet paper reveal the subtle charm of the mother and child theme in a moving position.*

38

Composition of three figures. These three brush and ink gesture drawings of a single model were executed in quick succession.

It was stated earlier that it is necessary to anticipate the ensuing gesture of the model. This, of course, is difficult at the outset, but with much practice it should improve in the future on-the-spot drawing. For example, a runner positioned in a starting stance will reveal taut muscles, but once he is sprung from the starting position these same muscles release their tension in a smooth rhythmic movement. Such portrayals demand alertness and confidence.

In suggesting and projecting gesture drawing to the early·adolescent it would be wise to initiate poses that are familiar to the student. A seated figure reading a book, a young girl holding a doll, two boys in a wrestling pose, a standing figure leaning on a shovel are poses that will

Group of figures (set of four drawings). Ink on wet paper and a limited drawing time allowed the student to express only the essential aspects of the personality.

40

lead the student more readily into an atmosphere of undisturbed concentration. Common activities readily experienced by the entire class will reduce the necessity for reinforcing the difficult poses to follow. If need be, a reversion to earlier poses to bring the class back into a feeling of security may be in order.

One must realize that gesture drawing is only one approach to drawing and that its definite purpose should be to strengthen one's expression. It would not, that is, be wise to continue the use of gesture drawing and forsake other approaches to drawing. One must utilize all the forces of art expression and adapt those that are most natural to the individual. Otherwise, the selected type becomes a dictatorial form of expression that will damage the artistic urge rather than deepen and strengthen it.

Therefore, the art educator must always be aware of those students who already possess an insight into the emotional and intellectual reactions of others.

Evaluation

Evaluating a gesture drawing is seemingly an easy task. Yet the more one involves himself in the process of gesture drawing, the more difficult is the process of evaluation. This is in part due to the time element. Brief time periods are essential for gesture drawing; for once the gesture is expressed, no other drawing is necessary. So it is especially important that the teacher realize that long periods of time for gesture drawing may destroy the incentive. The complexity of the stimulus, of course, determines the time span of the gesture drawing. Evaluation must then be based in the unification of the whole, in addition to the general mood or gesture of the stimulus. For example, the expression of a group of three individuals in different action poses must be evaluated on the basis of each individual gesture; but, more importantly, the three different poses must be related to each other to form a whole or a single unit.

Single figure (brush and ink). The strength of this drawing depends upon intense concentration on the model during a given time span.

42

Two figures (volume and gesture). The use of the wet paper method in drawing volume enabled a student to quickly "move into the pose;" spiral lines in a gesture drawing are a quick way to indicate the position of the model.

Furthermore, it is essential to evaluate the expression from the standpoint of the pure essence of gesture. Since the student must be equipped to act the role of the model in order that the gesture drawing have its most pronounced impact, it necessarily follows that evaluation must be based upon a close identity between student and model. For example, if the model projects the role of an anguished and suffering woman, the gestured expression must indicate identical emotional states. Any overplay of the gesture will have greater significance than others depending on personal experiences. This would be a disadvantage as well as an advantage. Familiarity with a pose sometimes causes anxiety, which, in

43

Combination drawing (gesture and contour executed on wet paper). Three minutes was allotted for the drawing of each of these four poses; the background idea was also timed.

turn, causes a tense expression. The student is then similar to the runner who realizes his capabilities and anticipates victory, but is disqualified for having left the starting block too soon.

The advantage lies in relaxation coupled with a personal "feel" for the gesture, assuming, of course, that the student is competent. Otherwise, familiarity with a particular pose would be of little benefit.

Evaluation then rests on the gesture that best identifies the action or mood of the model and on the suggestiveness, and yet the certainty of expression, that is gained through confidence.

44

Two single figures (brush and paint). Gesture drawing leads naturally into gesture painting; simple poses and a limited palette make the transition easy.

45

SUGGESTED ACTIVITIES

1. Draw simple standing and seated figures. Limit time of drawing to thirty seconds each.

2. Draw a single figure in action; begin with simple standing and squatting positions. Record the movement that takes place between the two positions.

3. Visit the gymnasium and draw the action of the participants.

4. While in a moving vehicle, try to draw the scene as it passes you by.

5. Draw a marching band.

6. Draw a runner as he runs around the track.

7. Draw the action of a football game.

8. Practice the gesture method by drawing objects not in movement. Limit drawing time to ten to thirty seconds.

9. Draw a person's hands as they move across the keyboard of a piano or typewriter.

10. Study the window washer at school; try to draw the movements as the brush moves vertically up and down the window.

DRADRAWING WEIGHT AND MASS 5

Drawing the human figure to reveal volume and weight differs considerably from the types of drawing previously discussed. Contour drawing deals solely with line, and gesture drawing deals with both line and weight but in a suggestive and indefinite manner. Now, however, the task is to exhibit weight and mass and simultaneously eliminate outlines. Outlines in this type of drawing are contrary to and unworthy of the drawing function, because their use stems from insecurities: the need to follow an oft-repeated pattern.

If the outline becomes so necessary that the student must rely on its use, then it is essential to reinforce the means by which this type of drawing becomes a natural part of the student's expression. This is indeed difficult. A sure approach is to permit the student to first express the stimulus in a line drawing, and upon its completion, direct his attention toward the elimination of the lines. This is accomplished by shading from one line to the opposite line that forms the shape in which the shading takes place.

The shading process sets the student at ease so that he works within an established area. Even then, difficulties arise, since particular areas of the figure of the object remain difficult to express. For example, it is a temptation to outline facial features; and once the outlines are placed, the student assumes that shading will "spoil" the picture. Furthermore, when shading does appear, it is a hesitant and reluctant approach and is not consistent with the whole of the figure. This is not unusual, because if the face is correct proportionately and satisfies the student, whereas other segments of the expression are to the contrary, a preoccupation with the expression of the face is indicated. Consequently, a "good" portrayal will be deemed "finished" or complete. The remainder of the figure then receives less attention; the student is willing to gamble with those areas and follow through with the prescribed assignment. It now becomes necessary to consider the whole expression and not merely segments. Furthermore, if the face is structurally incorrect and the student

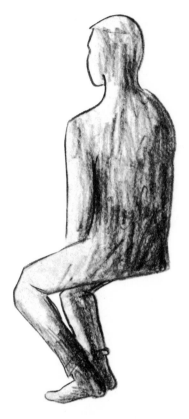

Simple seated figure.   Here an outlined drawing gradually gains weight.

is unaware that it is, then, conceivably, shading would be just as alien to his knowledge.

The second approach is more ideal but even more difficult to project, because the line concept of drawing has already been established.   The adolescent draws directly as the drawing reveals itself in solid blocky areas; he does so by using the broad side of the crayon.   As the crayon moves and develops each shape, it becomes necessary to consider the whole during the entire process.   Each section may be completed before proceeding to the next, or suggestion may indicate each area to which the student may return to complete in a more solid manner.

48

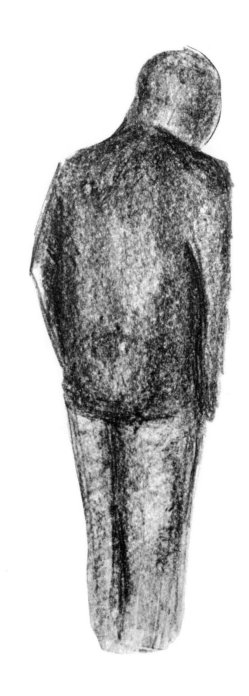

Simple standing figure. A simple pose evidences simple shapes; eventual darkening will make the figure more massive.

49

Standing figure. Weight and mass shading from dark to light indicate three-dimensional quality.

50

Single figure. A complex pose causes a variety of shapes, intensifying the problem of three-dimensional rendering.

One often encounters students who remain flexible and who prefer not to venture too far in any one direction. Such an approach is highly respected if the student understands the problem and realizes that mastering such a technique will not deepen or strengthen his natural way of drawing. However, if it is merely to shy away from a technique in order to "play it safe," then forceful motivation becomes necessary.

It is essential that the expression be identified in character with the stimulus, and in the direct approach this may be difficult because of the concentration centered upon each successive part rather than the whole. Yet in time, mastering this type of drawing will lead toward an intuitive approach that may become natural.

Group of two figures. Here solid forms eliminate outlines.

Evaluation

A point of evaluation is the absence of the outline; for if no outline exists, then it is evident that contrast of shapes exists by the application of dark and light—the expression is defined not by line, but by contrasting shapes. Again, as in all graphic expressions, the complexity of composition becomes a major factor of evaluation. Overlapping of figures, design within each figure, juxtaposition of the figures in relation to foreground and background areas, and identity of setting to the figures themselves are aspects of compositional complexity.

But, again, the specific evaluative factor is the release of outlines by the use of weighty and massive depiction of the natural stimulus coincidental with its gesture or position.

53

SUGGESTED ACTIVITIES

1. Using the side of a black crayon, shade an area from dark to light.

2. Shade with crayon or charcoal the receding and advancing areas of drapery.

3. With the side of colored chalk, draw a student model in a standing pose.

4. The cabinets in the art room would be a good stimulus for a broad, simple portrayal of volume and mass.

5. Using a simple cone, shade from dark to light.

6. Draw a series of cubes receding in space.

7. Draw a complete landscape of buildings, eliminating all outlines.

8. Draw a group of figures in block form; incorporate a background in like manner.

9. Draw a gesture of a group of students in limited time (three minutes).

10. Line up jars of paint of different colors. Use the sides of colored chalk and draw for contrast.

CONTRAST IN TEXTURE DRAWING

6

Knowledge of texture is frequently considered academic or intellectual. From a scientific view, it is. However, in extending a textural experience to the student, the result must encompass elements of art that expand the expression beyond scientific knowledge. As in all the arts, two major forces are at work. Knowledge gained through the visual stimulus can be expressed by careful preconceptual application or by intuitive application. Thus, it is necessary to alert oneself to the possibility of literal representation. In order to avoid it, the expression may lean toward a mechanical application of textural knowledge, but also lean toward an aesthetic arrangement of that knowledge.

So the problem here is not one of changing the approach of the student, but one of furthering and deepening the approach the student chooses to use. Dogmatic projection by the teacher will deter, and perhaps destroy, interest in further art experiences if persistence is employed. It is necessary that the teacher recognize the initial moves of the students so that an early adjustment can be made. There must be complete understanding of the approach used, and mutual confidence must prevail from the initial start to the final expression. In this way the student will not become confused in the process of manipulating textures simultaneously with tone contrast.

Before we proceed further, a discussion of the nature of the visual stimulus is necessary. Illustrations accompanying this chapter deal with the still life setup, but posed models would serve equally well and perhaps meet individual needs more accurately. Generally, however, the student will be more relaxed with the still life setup, since his inability to draw the human form would arouse his feelings of insecurity.

In arranging the still life, consider different types of textures: rough, soft, smooth, hard. Also consider unusual urns, chunks of tree branches, furs, skates. Arrange these materials so that different textures are adjacent to each other; thus, attention is directed to the still life. As the student expresses what is before him, his personality reveals itself in the

Still life setup (line and texture). This shows how a combination of line and solidly-textured areas compliment one another.

representation. He may express the visual stimulus objectively, and yet compose it aesthetically. Even though the textured areas are meticulously rendered—indicating an academic approach—the varying degrees of contrast in tone and in texture may result in an artistic expression. In addition, the relationship of line and space is a great force in determining this aesthetic result. This can be partly guaranteed by a sensitive arrangement of the still life setup.

In depicting the textured areas, the student must be consistent in the use of technique and tool. For example, if a fine quill pen is used within one area and a blunt lettering pen is used in another, it is necessary not only to balance such areas, but, more importantly, to use both tech-

STILL LIFE WITH CATTAILS. *Here the consistency of the pen lines retains the compositional setup.*

niques or tools in the same area. One should encourage various techniques in representing textures if and when the student is ready for them. Projection too soon would result in confusion and a disorganized expression. The use of pen and ink is mentioned because the accompanying illustrations were done in that medium. Brush, sponge, and other materials may be used to duplicate or represent textures, but the student must have control in their use and a knowledge of their effects. In addition to black and white, color may be used.

Because the materials are selected for the still life setup for their essential textural qualities, the student must diligently attempt to depict their nature. If he finds this too difficult, he may invent textures suitable to his personality.

57

STILL LIFE WITH CATTAILS. *The texture of natural objects demands a knowledge of nature as well as visual comprehension.*

58

Still life composition. This delicate pen work reveals charm and quietude; the pen lines are consistent.

The second major force of expression (intuition) seldom presents itself; but when it does, motivation must be geared to it and in a manner that will lead to deeper and greater expressions. How does one recognize intuitive qualities in an expression? Usually, the manner in which the technique is employed determines whether the response is intuitive. One must recognize a mechanical approach first in order to compare the two techniques. However, because an expression is nonmechanical does not indicate intuition. Also, an expression can be highly emotional and yet be nonintuitive, since intuition demands control. Intuition is insight through knowledge.

SINGLE BOWL OF FRUIT. *Contrast in tone is as necessary as contrast in texture.*

The mechanical technique can be identified by neatly applied symbols in a given area, such as cross-hatching of lines, tiny oval or circular shapes, duplicated grain textures of wood materials, and triangular shapes, or a combination of these things. Such application is preconceived and pretested. If the texture is an artificial one, the rendering must suit the shape to which it is applied. Furthermore, if the three-dimensional quality is employed, these same symbols must be used in an overlapping technique so that there is consistency throughout the area. If a second type of texture is employed in the same area, confusion may result because of the complexity of the visual stimulus, namely, the still life setup or the costumed model.

Intuitive execution of applied texture is not preplanned or pretested. Textures are applied at the precise moment that they are conceived. If a mistake occurs or a change of plans is indicated, the student immediately changes the style of texture. Furthermore, the three-dimensional quality

60

BOWL OF FRUIT WITH CATTAILS. *Three-dimensional qualities are reflected by shading techniques.*

is executed in a comparatively brief period of time, whereas in the mechanical approach, the entire area must be textured before consideration is given the "roundedness" of the area representing the visual stimulus. Furthermore, the intuitive response indicates a directness and perspective. The composition is conceived as a whole and executed directly—emphatically and fully—in as brief a time as possible to preserve the subjectivity that accompanies intuition.

It would be unwise to dictate either approach. It would be both educationally and artistically sound to perceive the personality, attitude, ability, and social adjustment of each individual and then challenge him with the approach best suited to his traits. If the intuitive response is not evident, then the mastery of the texture application should be guided into an aesthetic arrangement of textured areas. In any case, mastery or the accumulation of knowledge must never be the sole purpose of initiating any art experience.

Detailed composition of single objects. This intuitive composition has imaginative textures with accurate application.

Still life setup (line and texture). Here the emphasis on detailed textures contrasts with the complimentary lines.

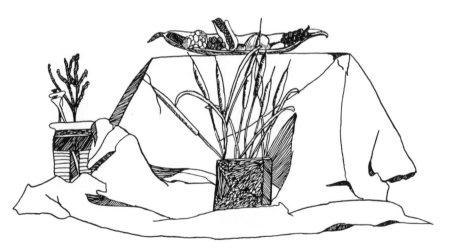

Evaluation

The texture drawing must be evaluated first by criteria set up to satisfy both approaches, but the underlying judgment in each case must be aesthetic: in the mechanical method, of the composition; in the intuitive method, of the character of the expression.

In evaluating a mechanical response, the teacher must realize that an aesthetic composition need not be formally balanced, nor must textured areas repeat. Nor need one evaluate the number or variety of textures represented. One must acknowledge the quality of a line, the placement of a textured area, the space surrounding a shape. Such evaluative factors may suggest an abstract portrayal. Line, mass, and space are abstract elements, but they do not necessarily indicate an abstract result. All elements of art are abstract symbols until they are used to represent something. Even then the representation may appear abstract. The use of these elements in constituting the whole in an aesthetic relationship is the determining factor in judging texture in a mechanical approach.

The intuitive texture experience must be an emotional depiction of the subject being expressed. The composition may be one of strength, delicacy, humility, or submission. To determine the abstract feelings of an individual is a difficult task. It is even more difficult to interpret the expression of such emotions. But to do so is the job of the art educator, and unless he is sensitive to the personal and social problems of the student and the personal trials in attempting to express these problems, an evaluation is not justified.

Seldom is the intuitive expression only partly that, whereas the mechanical method may reveal intuitive inclinations in particular areas of the whole expression.

Finally, one must always evaluate the whole. One cannot dissect the expression, evaluate each part, and then add the merits of the parts. A composition succeeds if each element reinforces every other element so that the result is one of complete unity.

SUGGESTED ACTIVITIES

1. Break open an apple; reveal its texture by drawing a part of it; a week later draw the same part of an apple.

2. Draw a closeup view of a gravel path.

3. Using ink wash and pen, draw draped transparent and opaque materials; render and texture for detail.

4. Draw and ink a coat rack with various types of coats. Stress the various textures.

5. Arrange various types of cloth on a bulletin board; overlap the different textures of cloth; render for contrast.

6. Arrange a still life using a variety of textured materials; render in ink line and ink washes.

7. Use costumed models representing different textures of clothing; render in watercolor and pen and ink media.

8. Take a field trip to study different natural textures (trees, grass, leaves, pavements, roots).

9. Choose from nature three or more contrary textures (rough-smooth) (curly-matted) (soft-hard). Try to duplicate these textures with pen and ink.

10. Draw two houses, one representing brick and one representing wood; use ink with pen to render the contrast of the two materials.

GEOMETRIC DRAWING : NONOBJECTIVE ART 7

Because of its apparent rigidity, the geometric drawing may indicate an academic or objective approach. Yet through further study one realizes the purpose and the depth involved in such an expression. "Geometric" is simply a term that identifies the origin of an approach to drawing. In geometry, certain symbols are used; examples are the triangle, square, circle, rectangle, and trapezoid. If one were to dissect nature, one would realize that the elemental shapes that constitute it are precisely such shapes, although modified in varying degrees. And so in using these "natural" shapes the student learns the basic structure of the things from which his idea evolves. The apparent abstract quality of the drawing is due not to an abstract way of thinking or doing, but to an elementary way of constructing one basic form upon another or dividing a basic form into numerous parts.

In projecting this form of drawing, it may be advisable to introduce only one mathematical symbol. If one desires, more challenging ideas may may be met by the use of numerous symbols interwoven.

Let us first consider the triangle. Two approaches are suggested. The first is to lightly sketch an idea to provide a starting point. After the sketch is complete or almost complete, alterations of the drawing are made in the form of triangles. As the drawing develops in detail, no segment of the idea should be destroyed. The idea must always remain recognizable even though it may appear abstract.

In order for the significant idea to be retained, additional lines are drawn to form additional triangles. These, in turn, serve two important purposes: 1) to reinforce the essential ideas through detail and 2) to introduce three-dimensional qualities by the use of dark and light. As more triangles are developed within a given area, the drawing begins to reveal a shading technique quite different from the common techniques.

The other approach is to begin with line directly and develop an idea as the lines move into space. The experience of "breaking space" with line is exciting, but when the lines make contact with others to

HOUSE WITH GARAGE. *The complexity of this composition demands a variation of triangular shapes.*

LANDSCAPE. *Drawing from nature enables the student to observe nature more accurately for details.*

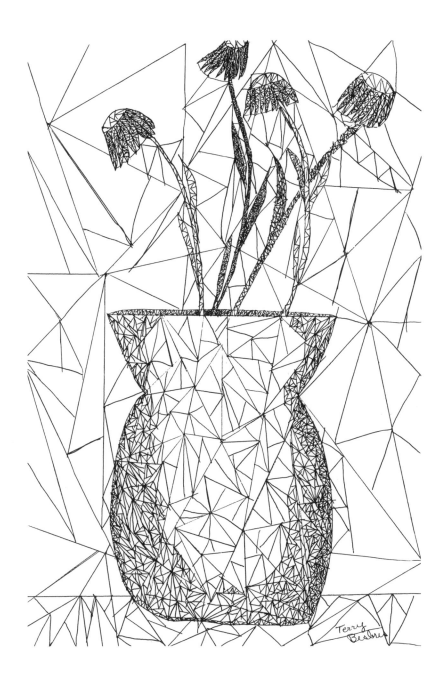

VASE WITH FLOWERS. *This imaginative vase of flowers reveals delicate and primitive qualities.*

form shapes, a new experience has developed. The ideas may be motivated in numerous ways, but stimuli of a visual nature should be provided.

Now let us examine more closely what actually happens in each approach. In the first, a model or still life setup may be used, and after the drawing is sketched in, the triangular development begins. This must proceed directly from the visual stimulus, namely, the model or still life setup, so that a proportionately correct structure is represented. For example, if a wrinkle is evidenced in the clothing of the model, the student then uses the wrinkle in initiating a new triangular shape. Furthermore, if the wrinkle indicates a receded area of the clothing, then that area is developed so that numerous smaller triangles form either a detailed area of texture or a three-dimensional quality of "roundness."

Incidentally, the wrinkle is caused by a change in the basic structure of the model. A change of posture will change the formation of clothing worn by the model, so the position of the model actually dictates the triangles to be formed.

In the final analysis the geometric drawing should closely represent the natural stimulus in its basic structure, revealing three-dimensional qualities, textured areas, details, receding areas, and shadows—all through the triangular process.

Because some students will prefer not to work from visual stimuli, they may initiate a design type of expression that develops as the idea enlarges or as the idea changes. A single line will begin the expression; and as each succeeding line breaks the space, an idea is extended into different directions. The expression may continue in the line concept with variations to indicate differences in quality. For example, as a line proceeds upward, a sudden change of direction will suggest or indicate a potential triangle. But it will also indicate a beginning of an "agitated" area, for a repetition of similar potential triangles will serve as a suggestion to return to this area and develop it into an idea. As the lines continue to break space, more potential triangles result and lead eventually to new ideas.

MAN WITH CIGAR. *Posed from life, this drawing indicates an intricate design of recessive areas; the darker the areas, the smaller the triangles.*

69

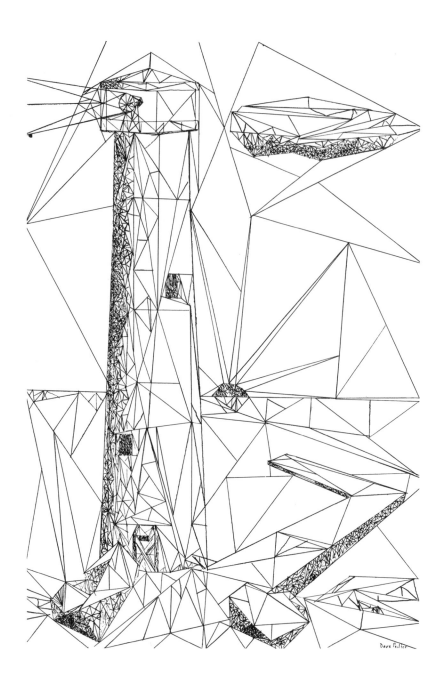

LIGHTHOUSE. *Here direction of line dictates the composition; ideas emerge as the design unfolds.*

70

Evaluation

Geometric drawing is evaluated by three predetermined purposes; maintenance of the original idea (in the second approach by its arrival), the handling of recessive areas, and the creation of three-dimensional quality.

In reference to an earlier statement that the original idea, once it is launched, must always be evident, it is also true that the final expression must reveal the initial idea but in a more rigorous manner. That is, not only must a house in the drawing retain its existence throughout the process of drawing, but its presence must be strengthened. If the idea is "lost" before the expression is complete, it must reinsert itself by means of the other two factors of evaluation; namely, an account of the recessive and three-dimensional areas. For example, a house has certain recessive parts, but if they are treated like parts that are not recessive, the image of the house will be difficult to ascertain. Consequently, application of the other evaluative factors would resolve this problem.

Proceeding further, one must account for each recessive area and determine if it is to recede as a flat surface or as a three-dimensional surface. Assuming that windows of a house set back into the house itself, the student then must break up the window areas into small triangles and the surrounding area of the house proper must be worked into larger triangles. The larger the triangles, the lighter the surface; the smaller the triangles, the darker the surface. This principle applies not only to flat areas, but to three-dimensional areas as well.

Actually, the basic evaluative factor is governed by its two necessary ingredients. The idea must never lose its identity, and its reinforcement and strength arise from the use of the triangular process of shading.

SUGGESTED ACTIVITIES

1. Draw with straight lines, breaking the space into an abstract design; eventually develop this into a drawing representative of nature.

2. Draw home furniture in triangular shapes.

3. By using mathematical symbols (square, triangle, rectangle) develop a drawing into realism.

4. Sketch a landscape and develop it into a triangular drawing.

5. Sketch a simple box, showing front, side, and top views. Divide into triangles showing contrast of each view; consider the shadow of the box as well.

6. Using a round three-dimensional object, show its roundness by shading with triangles.

7. Show recession of objects by setting up a simple still life.

8. Draw a single flower; study it for its geometric qualities.

9. Study a simple coffee cup; attempt to compose it into triangles.

10. Stack four or five boxes or books at different angles, one upon the other; draw and change to triangles.

ORIENTATION TO PAINTING   8

Stereotype symbols do not limit themselves to the area of drawing, since color presents its own kind of stereotype in the process of painting. In order to establish a sound approach and to curtail stereotype expressions, it is extremely essential to promote painting activities that meet individual needs.

Color must be conceived and executed in relation to an idea, and as the idea progresses so must the knowledge of color. Many art educators still cling to the isolated "color wheel" approach that often has stereotype results because the time span between the exercise of color wheel and the execution of an idea is too great. Unless the knowledge acquired is almost immediately applied to the idea expressed, the expression itself becomes academic, whether it represents nature abstractly or naturalistically.

Many students are highly emotional, and a teacher would be unjust in stifling an emotional outlet. That is why it is extremely difficult to acknowledge color relationships simultaneously with execution. But this must be done.

The painting experiences that follow are attempts to meet this important issue. However, it must be admitted that particular students may be "lost" in what is seemingly a rampage of "freedom"; students who have already mastered nature to a high degree and find that such experiences are unusual and distasteful to their ability must be individually motivated. It would be just as unwise to insist that such an approach to painting be followed by such a student as it would be to extend the color wheel method to those students who emotionally would not benefit. So one must recognize the individual differences in ability, temperament, and intelligence and gear painting experiences to meet more personal needs that will enable the students to express their emotions readily.

If one would consider the emotional outlet as the predominant purpose in art education, one would soon realize the ridiculous role academic approaches to expression play in the development of the student. One must appeal to the individual's sensitivity to color, which varies from stereotype representation of pure color to reckless execution of color, that has no boundaries. It is within this broad area that the art educators must work effectively with each student—inspiring, stimulating, probing, insisting, and encouraging each to adapt his expression to personal reactions to nature, both visually and emotionally.

Before proceeding further, it must be made clear what these individual needs are. It is essential at this moment to identify them in relation to ability, temperament, and factual knowledge. The student who repeatedly uses the pure color approach is aware of color in only limited application, either visually or emotionally, or both. An example may be as follows: The student initiates a landscape portrayal. The sky is painted blue—a pure color. The color white is not added to lighten the horizon, nor is a darker color added to intensify the overhead sky that occupies the top of the paper. The student knows that the sky is "blue," so it is painted blue, indicating a limited knowledge of color. Of course, one cannot rest here. Great painters have used the above approach with intelligence and emotional control. Precisely therein lies the difference. The student who applies pure color knows no other way. Repeated acceptance without realization of constant change becomes a stereotype when expressed.

Furthermore, the use of color depends largely on the complexity of design. If the sky area is pierced by numerous objects, a pure blue may appropriately be applied, whereas a large sky area painted pure blue will indicate a lack of ideas, which, in turn, is due to a low degree of intellect, a dearth of personal experiences, limited visual awareness, or an inability to express ideas.

It is now necessary to determine the cause of such expressions so that an individualized approach can be set in motion. Help may be had from the guidance director, teachers, and other school personnel in regard to intellectual capacities and emotional problems. Low intelligence is a primary cause, and with this in mind, the art teacher must plan experiences within the student's capacity, and must challenge him at all times.

Let us examine a painting that reveals large areas expressed in flat pure colors. Since the student lacks ideas to insert into his expression, he must incorporate color within areas already colored; that is, a sky area painted blue must now, in addition, be painted other shades of

74

blue or other colors so that the large area becomes an area of interest in itself. As a pure flat color it resembles a flat backdrop that appears to stand on end rather than recede into space. Perspective qualities are not essential, but the sky should reflect a high degree of emotion, whether it be calm and stately, or tempestuous and moving.

In most instances, the student of low intelligence will not comprehend the process of blending color. Thus, his expression will create a staccato impression; that is, broad, cumbersome strokes of paint would constitute that particular area in the initial stages of application. After primary acquaintance, this type of motivation is extended to all areas of the painting so that it will produce a consistency throughout the expression. It then is a matter of time until the expression comes under control. At first the expression will appear chaotic, but with time and practice, a simple idea may develop into a moving and dynamic expression.

With students of higher intellectual ability an approach through ideas would prove more inviting and more gratifying to both the student and the teacher. In such instances, the student is more capable of developing ideas to incorporate into his initial expression. Instead of having to be discouraged from using flatly painted areas, he can be expected to rely upon a reservoir of ideas to eliminate large areas. As each idea is inserted into the composition, ideas change to affect the presence of other ideas, and so eventually areas become related to others in size. Actually, a complex expression may be hampered by the inclusion of several colors within the same area because the complexity involved in the blending process may eventually dull the interest in reaching a conclusion.

Another stereotype symbol is the technical application of paint to an area of texture, such as grass or foliage. The result is an impression that leans toward decoration and superficiality. It is grass, dull and inactive. It may present an appearance of life, but it is not living. Nature should be meaningfully expressed, intuitively expressed. An illustration may clarify this point.

A student generally expresses an aspect of nature, such as grass, as an area or patch of a single color. He does not examine a blade of grass to determine its subtle variations of color. In order for these modulations to be intuitively expressed, they must be painted as singular units but conceived as a whole. If the student simply paints a mass of green and later superimposes upon it the minute aspects of nature, he has falsely expressed the nature of grass. A blade of grass possesses a life of its own, but a student sees grass as a whole and not as single units composing a whole.

To apply single units to an area that is complete in itself presents a sterile approach that does nothing to further the expression. The expression becomes a series of experiences that remain apart from each other even though they are evident in one painting. That is, what the student expresses intuitively must contain all the elements of his nature. Knowledge of nature must be incorporated into a painting at the time of creation. Otherwise, its application becomes a form of detachment rather than one of union.

The use of outlines in the expression may also be considered a stereotype if they occur repeatedly and if their use is due to a lack of knowledge or a lack of ability. The use of outlines is a carryover from an earlier stage of growth, when the child painted directly on the paper and "filled in" the outlined areas with color. As the child grows older, he continues this practice, but in reverse form. He does not paint natural objects by outlining. He realizes that objects differ in color and texture and that perspective and atmospheric conditions alter the appearance of nature. Yet he cannot accept the fact that it is precisely these differences that form the outlines.

Only a few of the predominant stereotype symbols that exist have been mentioned. To eliminate them, the student must be challenged in visual and emotional perception. It is hoped that the painting experiences in the following chapters may help to do this.

BRUSHLESS PAINTING 9

The approach used in brushless painting differs considerably from the direct approach to drawing discussed in the chapter on contour drawing. And it may seem illogical not to begin with painting that is similar to the drawing experiences. But since the emphasis is placed upon a different element, namely, color, it is essential that this element resolve itself in relation to ideas as soon as possible in order to eliminate future frustrations. Furthermore, in this particular experience, the student is not concerned with the development of observational powers; rather, he is concerned with broadening imaginative powers. Further, brushless painting sets the stage for all future painting experiences set forth in this book.

For want of a better term, "brushless" is tagged to this color experience because the initial move deals only with paint and wet paper. No brush is used. The experience involves a direct approach to painting in its application of the medium. Ideas materialize through suggestive qualities inherent in the painting, and they are completed through the application of textured and detailed areas of ink work.

Brushless painting has two major purposes: 1) to gain a greater knowledge of color in a nonacademic manner and 2) to initiate ideas through a comprehensive and detailed mixture of color, so that the eventual process of color mixture and accumulation of ideas is expressed completely and confidently. Academic approaches to learning about color often become remote in relation to an expressed idea, but what is more important, the knowledge gained about color has no immediate application to ideas. Thus detachment rather than attachment results. In brushless painting, color is understood through immediate blending so that ideas can be applied almost immediately, and with repeated performances ideas and color knowledge will be expressed simultaneously.

Instead of working from nature, one now works toward nature. Paint is dropped upon the wet surface of the paper. Different colors are applied to different areas of the paper. As the colors spread out over

LANDSCAPE. *Ink line accents "pull out" the idea from the colored washes.*

78

SWAMPLAND. *When a background color wash fails to suggest an idea, the inked design is executed using the background only as color.*

the surface and blend into one another to form other colors, ideas begin to flourish in the student's mind. The color yellow, spotted adjacent to the color blue, will blend into green to indicate an area of nature to be developed into grass or foliage. Similarly, the colors blue and red when placed side by side may suggest purple mountains in the distance. Various colors when blended may develop into a colorful bouquet of flowers.

With the initial stage of this experience complete, concern is given to the follow-up: the development of imaginative powers. Retaining suggestive areas as the painting proceeds to its conclusion is extremely rewarding, since the outcome depends almost entirely upon ideas discovered through the blending process. It is now time to apply these ideas to the colored background by using pen and ink. The brush may be used also if the painting suggests that the use would strengthen and promote the ideas.

At this moment of identifying ideas to express through suggestion, one must not be too anxious to extend the first idea through a series of ink lines. Instead, he should absorb ideas as he searches through the painting. After an extended tour, one eventually settles down to those ideas

STOCK CAR RACES. *This idea existed before the application of color; ink line and texture unify the entire design.*

HEADS AND BALLOONS. *Here the idea emerged after the application of color; the ink line was then applied as accents rather than outlines.*

COUPLE AT THE LAKE. *Here the idea was identified by opaque paint, as well as by the accents made with ink lines.*

81

that best suit his personality and that best indicate his loves and interests. As the ink is applied to the painting, one considers the suggestive qualities of the paint blend. The ink work should not be allowed to overplay its role. The color must still dictate the final result of the expression, so the overlaid ink work must make known or accent the ideas already existing in the painting.

A danger point that must be recognized is the temptation to outline the precise points at which the two or more colors make contact. If that mistake is made, suggestivity is defeated at the outset, and since the entire expression demands suggestive qualities throughout, it is imperative that the student give the expression the full benefit of the blending process. Furthermore, the outlining process indicates a lack of imagination if after exhaustive study the student succumbs to a "last-resort" technique.

The color and the ink must cooperate in the promotion of an idea. Also, the quality and character of the ink line must be suggestive and yet indicate quite firmly the idea to follow. Once this is established throughout the expression, detailed areas are developed to reinforce the idea. This reinforcement can be accomplished in various ways depending on the intensity and opaqueness of the colors. If the colors are dark and opaque, strong, bold lines would deepen and strengthen the expression. Delicate pen lines would contradict the initial stage of development of the expression, and such ink lines would be unworthy of the original power of the painting. So it is necessary that the basic color design and the overlay of ink work be similar in character and be consistently and firmly displayed. When the basic ink lines are suggested consistently

82

throughout the painting, thought and execution may be given to detailed areas.

If, for example, there is an area in which the colors blue and yellow are fused into green and which indicates the natural object "tree," one must consider the abstract areas in which the tree is to be expressed. The inked object must follow the suggested contour of the areas in which the colors blue and yellow formed the color green. If the area suggests an oak tree, a pine tree expressed in that area would contradict the idea suggested. Repeated practice of this kind would eventually lead to a wrong conclusion. A painting would result, but it would indicate a misunderstanding of the experience.

Also, in detailing an area, nuances of color should indicate the direction and character of ink lines within that area. And, finally, the completed composition must evidence a balanced relationship of color and line in conjunction with a direct relationship to idea. A series of isolated developments will reflect an isolated composition. The complete painting must be a complete expression, and an expression is never complete unless all units are conceived and executed as a whole.

Evaluation

Evaluation of any sort in the area of art should entail all the forces that make the expression worthwhile. These include both emotional and intellectual forces in balance so that each strengthens the other. But specifically, the brushless painting must further be evaluated by the purposes it set out to serve.

TREE. *Here the surface of the white paper acts as the design element; the form of the tree is inked over the colored wash background.*

84

Evaluation must first be based on the knowledge of color that is in evidence in the final expression. This aspect of evaluation may be difficult but one must realize that the knowledge is not gained through a single expression but is accumulated over a definite span of time. The final result or the ultimate expression should reveal a progression of knowledge procured through the blending process. If the expression reveals a retention of colors, such as green, brown, orange, grey, and purple, that are formed by other colors, evaluation is then based upon the use of ink work to reinforce the ideas stemming from the placement of the blended colors.

A factor to consider in this regard is the destruction of an area by overplaying the ink application. If this overplay happens, the expression will be of a low caliber. On the other hand, if insufficient strength is placed on the original color blend by use of the ink application, the student then has overlooked the connection of the two elements working together. The color must always dictate what is to follow. Otherwise, the expression serves no purpose. The experience becomes one of another nature.

A final evaluative factor is the composition of the emotional and imaginative qualities that stem from the individual personality. If the original application of color is strong and intense, the follow-up of ink work must coincide; if the initial color blend is subtle and delicate, the overlay of ink will dictate and reveal the personality of both the expression and the expressor.

SUGGESTED ACTIVITIES

1. Apply various colors of tempera paint to wet paper; allow paper to dry. Let colors suggest various ideas to be developed, first with ink line and then with ink textures.

2. Arrange a still life setup. Wet a paper and apply color to the paper in an attempt to quickly duplicate the still life.

3. Apply color to a wet paper in a circular movement; develop with ink line into a bouquet of flowers.

4. Using the above method, develop a theme of children holding balloons.

5. Apply color to wet paper in a broad vertical movement; develop with ink line into an architectural site.

6. Close your eyes and daydream for five minutes; after wetting the paper, attempt to transmit the daydream to the paper. Ink lines may serve to accent ideas.

7. Listening to and interpreting music may initiate ideas with color; followup with ink lines, that should coincide with the color layout.

8. Apply cool colors to wet paper to suggest moods of loneliness, peace, quietude. Ink in ideas that are identified with the mood.

9. Apply warm or hot colors to wet paper to suggest moods of anger, heat, fire. Ink in ideas that are identified with the mood.

10. Study the paintings of Miro, Klee, and Kandinsky as a background or followup. Indicate the ideas and philosophies of these renowned artists.

WATERCOLOR PAINTING 10

Watercolor has for years been considered an elusive painting medium, yet this "elusiveness" has generally been reflected by the adult mind. No serious artist would abandon watercolor expression simply because it was too difficult. For if the watercolor expression can deepen and enrich an idea more than any other form of creative experience, then the artist feels the need to master the medium. With this thought, the student must be invited to explore the potentialities of watercolor. If the process is indeed too difficult, the student must realize that through concentrated effort.

Because of its flexibility, one may consider watercolor ideal for student use, but problems mount as the student becomes more involved. The impossibility of erasing mistakes is the major frustration. Other difficulties will be discussed in relation to the three different approaches suggested in this chapter.

Competent watercolorists arrive at a precise technique after years of experimentation. The student must have explicit directions in his approach; for freedom of expression can come only with mastery of the medium, in a limited sense. Limitation has to do with mastering one of the three techniques that follow.

Let us consider the first approach, that of transparent application. From the first application this seems easy, since water is first spread over the area to be painted. While the paper is still wet, paint is added so that the water and paint fuse. At this point the student is confused, delighted, or disgusted. Being unready for this collision, the student is stymied. Even if he is warned of it, he is not apt to believe it until he sees it. In handling watercolor in this manner, one must realize that the water is the working agent and that color is the indicator of the emotional quality. Thus, water must be used in controllable fashion. If too much water is applied to the surface, puddles form in areas on the paper and cause a deadening effect. Experience will eventually dictate the amount of water to be used in a given area to control these water hazards.

LANDSCAPE. *Spots of white paper act as accents of color in this complex composition.*

Associated with the problem of excess water is that of wet areas adjacent to areas being painted. Colors fused unintentionally frequently cause the student to give up in disgust. This is especially true if his composition is complex in nature. If such frustration persists, it would be advisable to apply paint to the surface first, and add water while the paint is still wet. As the water touches the paint, the two will fuse in a more controlled fashion. In other words, it is easier to control the area if water is added to the painted area rather than paint to a watered area. As for proceeding to other areas, the student must realize that one area must be dry before an adjacent area is painted.

Of course, with a growing mastery of this approach, the intentional fusion of adjacent color areas will expand the freedom of the student.

88

The expansion of freedom should reflect a greater insight, a more humble approach to humane ideas, and a deeper emotional reaction toward nature. Technical mastery must never sacrifice the emotional content and the compositional elements that bring it about.

The second approach is the use of the paper as accenting lines or areas or as a color (white) in itself. In projecting this type of watercolor expression, the teacher's motivation should stem from visual stimulus. With his attention focused on a given object, the student will more readily relate aspects of the stimulus to appropriate areas on the paper. For example, a model positioned to indicate numerous folds or creases in her clothing will be painted by allowing white parts of the paper to act as highlights or accents. The white paper can also act as a form in itself by simply painting shadow to define the form.

HOUSE AND BOAT. *Here watercolor paint was used in an opaque manner; the dry brush technique was also utilized.*

BACKYARD. *The white surface of the paper was used to indicate the actual object of the fence; colored washes were used to advantage.*

90

In this method little paint is used in order to utilize the white paper to its fullest. One of the danger points is the sharp contrast formed by the white area and the abrupt brushstroke. If unintentional, it frequently reveals an agitated area exhibiting distractive elements. In order to correct or tone down this agitated area, a brush load of water is carefully spread over it. Also, if the student becomes overconscious of the inclusion of white areas (as he may in the beginning), he may fail to define the forms of the expressed objects. If such is the case, he may spread over the entire surface a neutral color to unite the isolated areas.

Finally, the placement of white areas should be consistent in arrangement to reflect a natural form of expression; that is, white areas should be conceived objectively but expressed intuitively. At this stage of growth, intuitive expression is difficult, but if the student does not work toward a mastery of his tools so that this intuitive response asserts itself, his expression will always be one of complacency and sterility.

A third technique—(there are others)—that may assist the student is the directed lean toward opaqueness. Opaqueness being the opposite of transparency, the student may find it easier to make the transition from familiar tempera painting to watercolor. The student who has mastered the building-up process of tempera paint will find that building up watercolor is not too different. However, the major difference is that watercolor must never reach the stage of complete opaqueness lest its beauty be defeated. In building up the watercolor in this manner, the paint-laden brush may be applied to a wet surface or a dry surface. However, more satisfying results will stem from a moist surface. Moreover, the paint must always remain transparent. After the first layer is dry, a slightly darker color is added, but it also must be transparent so that both layers of paint are visible. The second layer may indicate shadows, textures, or three-dimensional qualities. The more layers of paint added to the expression, the more body is given to the painting.

As the painting darkens, the spirit of the expression deepens. This statement suggests the age-old argument that watercolor painting never reaches the depth of emotional and spiritual experience that is found in oil paintings. This is not necessarily true. However, one might say that because of the short execution time of a watercolor, little opportunity is allowed for reflection or contemplation during the actual process of

CONTEMPLATION. *Opaque and transparent watercolors were used to promote the idea; transparent washes toned down the background buildings.*

92

FATHER AND SON. *This gesture painting utilized transparent and opaque washes and line to promote the idea.*

93

STILL LIFE. *Here the still life setup dictated the arrangement and color to be used.*

painting. This is not so of oil painting, or for that matter, of casein or tempera painting. Thus, the leaning toward opaqueness of this water-color approach will heighten and enrich the spiritual quality of the expression that should be the ultimate goal of watercolor painting. Frequently, however, it is nothing more than an exercise or an experimental problem.

Each of the above-mentioned techniques of watercolor painting is proposed and geared to the personality of the student in order to fully develop artistic potential.

Evaluation

Each watercolor approach should be evaluated on the technique itself in relation to the idea. For example, if the wash technique is used, consistent application of the wash should be evident, and the idea should be brought to its fullest strength. The presence of opaque areas indicates a lack of control that may weaken the idea because of adverse attention. Consistency reflects unity and order. Yet one must realize the flexibility of the student in judging his work, so that in the learning process he should be allowed time to near a mastery of his particular approach. In the educative process one must not judge too soon with a beginning medium. Yet since evaluation is necessary, not only the existing work but also the potential should be judged.

In any of the three methods, the transparent quality must always be evident even though it may verge on opaqueness. The transition from the formal technique of tempera painting to watercolor expression is frequently difficult for the student. Consequently, opaque qualities are evident in the first trials. This may be cause for a low evaluation, but as these areas are slowly exchanged for transparent areas, the evaluative factor becomes more positive.

The student when confronted with a different medium of expression often absorbs himself with technique, thus sacrificing composition and emotion. An evaluation must never be based on technique alone; for technique is merely a means to an end. Technique is the creed of the painter, but only because it is incorporated with composition and emotion. The three must never be separated. Even though the three elements are a unity, at times one must evaluate them separately.

At all times the student must express an idea with technique. Emotion is intuitive, and the composing of an idea should also be intuitive. In fact, all forces that constitute an artistic expression should act simultaneously. The work should be judged by its unity, yet it is sometimes necessary to judge it by its separate merits.

SUGGESTED ACTIVITIES

Suggested themes to be painted:

1. An old house high on a hill
2. An ancient tree in the country at dusk
3. Sand dunes
4. Cottage on the lake
5. Surfboarding
6. Residential neighborhood
7. Sunning on the beach
8. Still life
9. A rainy day
10. Faces

VARIATIONS IN INK 11

The various techniques with the ink medium perhaps deserve little attention, and yet the art teacher may not realize the potential of the medium. Ink is frequently thought of in terms of lettering, posters, scratchboard, book cover designs, and the like. It is always a means to an end, seldom an end in itself. Yet occasionally, one has the experience of witnessing the result of ink doodling. It presents to us a certain charm, or a feeling of fantasy. Then comes the horrible mistake of subjecting an entire class to this newly discovered expression, on the assumption that if one person is successful, others will be also. A more definite conclusion may be that the success of the student indicates a greater and longer experience with this medium. He has discovered its potential, the teacher has not. However, the experience of discovery may be the initial move toward an awareness and an understanding of the particular student and of the potentialities of the medium itself.

But one does not merely set up an experiment with the ink process. This will only lead to frustration, and perhaps a dead end, before the full benefits of the ink medium can be realized. Ink must be used in conjunction with an idea. It is not enough to merely "get the feel of it." Time and effort will eventually result in its mastery. The ink expression is an art form in itself. It is not a mere experience, but a series of experiences. It is a way of expression, just as oil painting is or as sculpture is. It is the finding of a medium that will best express an idea. This, of course, may be said of all media.

Yet ink has been generally sidelined and brought into play only to meet the needs of the school for posters or as lettering exercises. It is time that the medium of ink be displayed as an art form expressing excitement, charm, and solemnity.

Illustrations accompanying this chapter stem from visual stimuli, from memory, and from doodling. But in most cases, a mastery of the ink technique is evident. Let us discuss the tools with which ink is applied. Some of the more popular ones are the quill pen, the lettering

In My House. *This detailed study of objects includes a self-portrait; emphasis was on texture, perspective, and three-dimensional qualities.*

pen, the commercial ballpoint pen, the brush, and the sponge. The three most successful approaches are pen and ink, brush and ink, and a combination of the two.

The beauty of ink can be realized in the character of a line as evidenced in contour drawing, in the movement of multiple lines as witnessed in gesture drawing, in the appearance of texture as revealed in texture drawing, and in the accent of form as evidenced in brushless painting.

98

LONELINESS. *Here various poses rendered in contour reveal the student's ability to arrange figures to express an idea.*

The realization of each of these specific expressions is brought about by constant and selective motivation.

Since the ink expression accompanies an idea, it is necessary that the student determine the best means of expressing the idea. Thus, he must concern himself with the tool prescribed for him. In the case of contour drawing the ballpoint pen is ideal because its flexibility allows the ink line to move in all directions with ease. In the case of gesture drawing

IN THE LIBRARY. *Ink wash and gesture lines produced this strongly emotional head; its strength is retained by an appropriate background.*

the ballpoint pen works equally well. Gesture drawing calls for quick, intuitive lines, and the ballpoint is a perfect slave to this type of expression.

For more precise and calculated ink work, such as the texture and geometric variety, the quill pen and the lettering pen will prove more successful, because the execution is generally preconceived.

The use of the ink medium is not limited to the expression of line. The student will find that ink wash will surmount the initial barrier of penetrating a blank surface. It is a simple matter to wet the surface

100

DESPAIR. *The simplicity of this drawing was made powerful by the use of strong washes for contrast.*

before applying an ink wash. Immediately minimized is the fear of making mistakes. Also, the wash establishes a middle ground between black and white. From this point on, the ink line is related to the surrounding background. This is an excellent approach to inking architectural landscapes as well as on-the-spot inkings of sporting events. The ink wash indicates body or volume, and the line defines its form.

Another use of ink seldom exhibited is its incorporation with tempera or watercolor paint. Some art educators still cling to the belief

MEETINGPLACE. *Various tones of ink washes unified the background for these posed figures.*

that a medium designed for a particular use must be used by itself. This may well be, but it does not preclude the possibility of enriching the expression by the use of a second medium. An ink line as accent and the color within a painting are a valid combination. Not only does the combination reinforce an idea, but its continued use in a flexible manner may lead to a form of expression suitable for particular students.

The sponge technique has a legitimate use in expressing textural effects, but here again the student must be careful not to become a slave to the material used. Frequently, teachers have permitted and perhaps

CLASSROOM. *Strong horizontal background planes unite the vertical lines of these posed figures; line, texture, and washes were used.*

even welcomed the use of "junk" material as a diversion or an experiment that in most instances proved to be fun without learning. The attempt is to stimulate learning by quick response. Unfortunately, the enthusiasm is short-lived because the goals set forth are shallow, and the materials used are novelties that stunt the creative growth of the student.

So, in any ink experience, proven materials should be used because they have been designed to do specific jobs. The accompanying ink drawings are examples of the proper use and motivation of the ink expression.

CRUCIFIXION. *Brush, pen, and ink produced an emotional depiction of the crucifixion theme in this sketch from life.*

Evaluation

An art expression executed in ink must be evaluated by the emotional quality brought about by the particular technique of line, wash, or both. Judgment must also be made on the purpose of each. The use of ink wash and line must correspond to the idea; that is, the wash must represent an area, and the line must represent the form of the area. Reference is not to an outline, however, since an outline would defeat the purpose of the combination. The ink wash must also include tones of black to light gray, indicating recessive areas or perspective. For example, a building with receding parts would demand different tones of gray. Windows are set back into the house proper, and the ink wash should indicate this by a slightly darker shade than the directly adjacent side. The ink line, if used, must accent the edge of these two areas.

In the area of gesture and contour drawing each must be judged quite differently. Since line is used to develop observational powers in contour drawing, excessive lines would lower the evaluation. Also, the complexity of the composition and the intellectual and emotional qualities are factors to be considered. On the other hand, gesture drawing is based on the recording of gestures evident in the visual stimulus. The flexibility of the ink line in registering these gestures is one of the evaluative factors. Again, however, each line must express meaning.

Finally, the ink expression should reflect an inner significance, an idea fully expressed. Otherwise, the possibility of the ink process may once again be relegated to the job of subsidiary art projects.

SUGGESTED ACTIVITIES

1. Draw from a student model. Using wet or damp paper, apply ink line with pen or brush in recording the model. Limit the time to two minutes.

2. Using the above method, draw three or more figures as a single composition; add background.

3. Using ink washes, indicate segments of the posed models. When dry, apply ink lines to identify the models.

4. Using ballpoint pen, illustrate or draw movement or action as seen at a sporting event (football, basketball, track, soccer). Limit time to two minutes.

5. Draw a still life setup stressing textures of various materials.

6. Draw a group of three or more figures (student poses), one at a time, and arrange them into a composition to suit individual needs. Complete the background. Ink the entire composition in line first. Add ink washes and textures to complete the composition.

7. Using a black ink felt pen, draw quick gestures of moving figures; add a background.

8. Draw a still life or landscape; ink in artificial textures.

9. Ink with brush a playing orchestra, indicating the vertical, horizontal, and diagonal lines.

10. Apply various shades of ink washes to white paper. Purposely allow certain large areas of white paper to remain untouched. Draw in contour three or more figures both in the wash areas and the white areas so that the ink contour unites the white to the wash areas. Complete the composition with an appropriate background.

STILL LIFE AND LANDSCAPE PAINTING 12

Painting the Still Life

Many students of art and artists themselves regard the painting of still life as dead subject matter. The lack of emotion and movement and the possibility that greater aesthetic experiences result from subject matter that is more personal are usually given as reasons. An expression of the still life can be personal or impersonal; it can be regarded as a means to an end or an end in itself.

Still life painting is often considered as discipline in learning the fundamentals of painting and drawing. Color, composition, contrast, and texture are generally considered the elements necessary for an evaluation of the still life painting. The still life is frequently treated as an exercise, and as such it can move dangerously toward an academic approach. Then it may indeed be regarded as a dead subject, lacking emotion, and concerned solely with acquiring the principles of painting. It is true that these principles must be acquired, but as an end in themselves they serve no purpose in the realm of creative accomplishment.

Still life must be approached boldly and directly, if it is to benefit the student emotionally. It must free the student to experiment, think, select, and reinforce his thoughts discriminately. The student must feel the need to go beyond the visual aspects of the still life setup.

Ideas become buried within the individual through lack of self-confidence, and art educators frequently feel that a technical process accompanying a direct approach better satisfies a student. That is, creative processes such as etching, lithography, and enameling absorb the student in the technical process so much that the direct approach to an expression is sidelined and made subordinate to the technique of projecting that idea. For example, drawing is a direct approach to expressing an idea. Etching is drawing; but because there are the frequent interruptions of technical and chemical reactions, the idea is no longer foremost, nor can it be until the process is so mastered that it becomes

STILL LIFE THROUGH A WINDOW. *The original still life stimulus
was altered to suit the emotional reaction of the idea.*

STILL LIFE WITH FLOWERS. *This still life setup is characterized by
the emphasis on the flower pattern evident in the posed drapery.*

synonymous with the idea. Such activities are strongly advocated by art educators, but if physical facilities for them are lacking, other activities must be available. One such activity is the still life.

Several approaches to the still life have been used successfully, but two should suffice here, since they attempt to direct the student to an imaginative and zealous interpretation of nature. A still life is not really dead if the individual portraying it is properly motivated. The objects of a still life are objects of nature that have been plucked from the stream of life, or they are objects that were made by man. Even so, such man-made things as vases were at one time clay—a living, moving part of the earth's surface. There is no reason why these natural objects should not be resurrected from their static positions in life.

A first method is the accumulation of numerous natural objects selected by the teacher, placed in an informal setup to be viewed by the students. The teacher may suggest that the students paint the entire arrangement as presented or rearrange the setup to suit the majority of the class. If such an approach is discouraging to a particular student, the teacher can suggest, "You need not paint all the objects, but only those that please your eye." Some students will attempt to duplicate the actual colors of the objects. Others will modify colors or change them completely in order to satisfy their emotional reaction to color. Still others will add textures that are nonexistent. But all of these modulations are extending the still life beyond the lifeless position it holds. Concern is given not to an exact duplication, but only to an emotional expression, which naturally binds itself to a personal composition. Frequently, through motivation of this nature, students will acquire objects and arrange them in a fashion suitable to their own personalities, and thus the interest is heightened.

The second approach is more subjective, but it is, in actuality, an extension of the first, since it calls for an expression extending beyond the initial stimulus of the still life setup. The first method is an invitation to paint an arrangement of natural objects. Freedom exists within the framework of the visual, and in some instances subjective paintings will result. However, with the second approach a pronounced attempt is made to incorporate objects of nature that will develop or reinstate the imaginative power of the individual. The student now uses objects that suggest imagery and fantasy. Here the problem is to make these natural

STUDY. *A limited palette created this emotional expression; simple objects were used.*

110

BOTTLES. *In this gesture painting of an imaginary still life, black ink lines accent the objects.*

objects transcend their static position and become imaginative and suggestive expression. Such objects as chains, rope, fruit, bones, rocks, and plants become symbols of an imaginative expression. It is difficult to approach objectively an idea that results in a subjective release. This is not necessarily the task. The objects are selected by the students to further and to deepen ideas; they are suggestive of events immediately concerned with the student. The idea is objectively approached, but the actual process of painting that idea is a subjective one.

Some students are incapable of subjectively expressing an idea. But if nothing more is gained, those students will possess a greater knowledge of nature and its beauty, and we need the appraisers as well as the creators of beauty.

STILL LIFE WITH PITCHER. *This intuitive painting of a still life arrangement reveals the student's tremendous ability to alter ideas in "midstream."*

112

STILL LIFE WITH BOWL OF FRUIT. *Consistency of technique is reflected in this still life painting which shows a direct intuitive approach.*

MOONLIGHT. *This residential home was altered to suit the emotional theme of abandonment.*

114

Landscape Painting

Visual stimuli have motivated many of the prescribed types of drawing and painting mentioned in this text, and such stimuli are further introduced in the outdoor scene.

The student must now approach the business of landscape painting as an emotional outlet rather than the generally accepted philosophy of acquiring factual knowledge: that of seeing and expressing the compositional element of perspective. Perspective now comes into existence incidentally. It is through the direct approach to painting that emotion is expressed almost intuitively and from which the compositional elements naturally flow.

The suggestion has been made that the element of perspective is eliminated from the practice of landscape painting. This is not literally so. The problem of perspective is forgotten during the process of painting, but it is not eliminated. Perspective in the process of creation, if it is considered solely and objectively as the underlying force of expression, is a hindrance to a deeper and more interpretative meaning of nature.

The mastery of landscape painting is preceded by a discriminatory method of locating a good compositional scene. Hopping from one site to another must be discouraged. Landscape painting demands contemplation of the scene to be expressed. Roaming the landscape is a form of contemplation—one is seeking the ideal. "Hopping" refers to the practice of preparing oneself to paint and then suddenly realizing that a more suitable site perhaps exists elsewhere, and one moves to another location. Constant relocating leads to futile results, because concentrated effort of visual perception has been avoided.

115

HOUSES AND TREES. *A limited time produced this quick, exciting,
intuitive expression of trees and houses.*

COUNTRYSIDE. *This landscape was painted from memory; paint
was applied quickly, and mistakes were "erased" by painting new
ideas or changing the old.*

WHEATFIELD. *This is an expressionistic approach to a simple theme.*

Roaming the landscape will demand more time, but the results will be more intellectual and more emotional. The more one absorbs the landscape, the more personal the experience of expressing it becomes. And when the student finally "digs in," he is prepared emotionally and intellectually to survey the landscape and record it artistically.

Landscape painting is not only a complete expression in itself, but it is complete without the preliminary process of drawing. Predrawing or presketching a painting is one of the most difficult processes to overcome. Yet, overcoming it is necessary in the procedure advocated here. By a preliminary sketch is meant the type of drawing that records detail, textures, indications of color relationships, and in general, is a practically complete composition. It is preliminary only in the sense that it sets the stage for the painting to follow.

117

House with Red Chimney. *An unusual application of paint created this exciting expression of an on-the-spot scene.*

Trees. *A combination of tempera and enamel caused this strong expression; the scene was drawn quickly in pencil, dripped over with black enamel, and then tempera paint was applied.*

When the student expresses the landscape in the preliminary sketch, he absorbs himself in a personal reaction to the scene. The painting that follows is prescribed by the notations of detail, texture, shadow, and color. Why is it that many students refuse to paint scenes that they have sketched? The answer generally is, "Because I will spoil it if I paint it." This is true. Painting will spoil it, because the functions of drawing and painting are separate, and consequently the results are separate when they should be one and the same.

Such an attitude is accounted for by the unrelatedness of the drawing of a scene and the painting of it. The moment the drawing exists, there exist boundaries within which the paint is applied. If the paint is not applied properly and accurately within these limits, the student rebels is disgust, and frequently he refuses to paint. But even more important is the stifling effect on the student—not the unwillingness to paint the scene he has drawn, but rather the "closing in" of his personality by dampening his emotional reaction to the scene in continuing to paint in this manner.

On the other hand, preliminary sketches, if they are kept suggestive and if they are utilized by students who know their function, often serve a good purpose.

Evaluation

The direct approach to landscape painting may be evaluated on a number of points ranging from extreme suggestiveness to complete definition as long as the paint is applied directly and intuitively. In other words, painting with suggestive qualities having various interpretations are as valid as paintings that specifically define each visually comprehensible item, provided artistic content is not sacrificed in either case.

SUGGESTED ACTIVITIES

Still Life Painting

1. Paint directly a still life setup, eliminating preliminary sketching. (Should be completed in one or two hours.)

2. Place an assembly of unusual objects on a chair; have students choose only certain objects and arrange them into a good compositional expression.

3. Arrange a still life of flowers, vase, bowls of fruit; paint the setup and incorporate a natural background.

4. Arrange still life objects stressing contrast in textures.

5. Arrange objects suggesting fantasy (gloves, slippers, bones, oil lantern, chain). Paint objects into a composition, allowing the objects to suggest psychological or symbolic meanings.

Landscape Painting

6. Paint from memory an impression of an outdoor scene (woods, seashore).

7. Paint a single tree or other plant life on a barren landscape to indicate a mood of loneliness.

8. Paint an old building or alleyway to indicate a mood of decay or poverty.

9. Paint a picture combining a rich and poor settlement area.

10. Paint a close-up view of nature emphasizing texture (tree trunk, branch, corner of building).

OTHER MEANS OF EXPRESSION 13

Tempera Painting

Rather than discuss ideas in the area of tempera painting, we shall introduce techniques, since the technique of applying paint generally indicates personality and individuality, not so much conveying ideas in themselves as suggesting personal and emotional reactions to ideas.

Although tempera is a water-base paint, opaque use of it enables the student to change techniques in midstream, thus strengthening or subordinating an idea. This can be done by three major methods: 1) by allowing the water to act as the moving agent so that the paint in its application can be moved about to suit the character of the idea, 2) by mixing paint directly upon the surface by applying a second color while the first is still wet so that the colors move into one another and simultaneously build up the surface, and 3) by applying a dry-brush technique to a completely dried surface. Each of these types of painting with tempera must be examined more closely.

In applying water to the surface to be painted, technical problems should be at a minimum so that the process of painting is not hampered. If too much water is applied to the surface, it creates flooded conditions on the paper so that the paint, when applied, becomes uncontrollable; that is, the paint sets on top of the water and does not penetrate the surface. On the other hand, if too little water is applied, the surface area may dry before the paint is added to or mixed with the water. Time and practice will resolve this problem.

As the paint is applied to the wet paper, the student considers other colors to be used in the same area. For example, a sky area will demand the color blue. So in applying blue to the moist area, the other colors must now be added. If the student is depicting a gray, gloomy day, colors that indicate this emotional state are added to the blue sky area. The colors black and white mixed with blue will cause this transformation.

THE HUNTER. *In this intuitive painting, paint was applied to cover the original ideas; paint was applied directly without a pre-sketch.*

122

FIGURE WITH RED BACKGROUND. *Here enamel was dripped to form an image of the posed technique; the tempera paint was applied with a palette knife. This technique often results in a dynamic portrayal of an idea.*

WAITING FOR A BUS. *This idea was sketched out carefully from life; the colors were pre-mixed before application to the surface.*

PICKING FLOWERS. *This figure was drawn from a model; the application of paint activated the idea.*

Here we have considered only one area of a given painting. Areas adjacent to the sky present further problems. For example, if the sky area remains moist while paint is applied to an adjacent area, colors will blend unintentionally. What appears to be a minor mistake frequently causes the adolescent to give up. Ironically, this "mistake" when executed intentionally creates effects that appear accidental but have occurred because there is a thorough knowledge of the medium and mastery of manipulation.

Another problem resulting from this approach is the disorganization of the entire expression. This occurs when concentrated effort is placed upon individual areas with little concern for future progress. Even though each succeeding area reveals a mastery of technique, unless the entire whole reveals a union of all its parts, the expression fails.

The second approach, which involves direct mixing and application of paint to a dry surface, causes problems of a different nature. Freedom of paint movement is limited somewhat by the dry surface of the paper. In place of the water agent, the paint itself acts as the moving agent. So it is essential that the paint contain a considerable amount of water when applied. A frequent frustration of this technique is the "drying up" of an area so that blending the color becomes impossible unless the entire area is repainted. This may lead to cracks in the painted surface because of numerous layers of paint.

One of the major problems of the student in painting is his inability to express intuitively an idea complete in itself. Concentration is focused upon segments of the composition so that complete unity is seldom evident. Spontaneous expression at this age level is not uncommon, but intuitive thinking and expression are infrequent. One may spontaneously express an emotion, but the complexity of thought and emotions interwoven into a single portrayal demands an intuitive mind. Thus, a painting is initiated and completed in a process that is concerned solely with the fulfillment of an idea. As the reader has perhaps realized, this is possible only if one has mastered the knowledge and rendition of color so that color becomes a servant to his touch.

GREEN RIVER. *This unusual selection of color reveals an emotional reaction to the scene depicted; the paint was mixed directly on the paper.*

126

THE WINDSTORM. *The slant of these figures indicates the strength of the storm; facial and bodily gestures add to the idea.*

SISTERS. *The impressionistic style of painting solves problems of shading, recession, and three-dimensional qualities.*

THE OUTING. *This entire composition was painted directly from the original scene; this demands a thorough knowledge of color.*

128

An important distinction must be made here. A student may indicate an intuitive response to nature without having the evident mastery of color. To paint intuitively, one must be in command of the color process. Furthermore, the application of this knowledge must be simultaneous with one's emotional reaction to an idea. It is conceivable, however, that this mastery of color is momentary, that it is experimental at the precise time it is applied to the surface. Also, the student is not at all sure that the colors he applies are going to create the effects he wants.

The important thing to remember is that although the student is not sure of the outcome at the time of application, he is indeed confident that the outcome will satisfy him. In this regard the immediate application of paint may result in mistakes that are soon erased by the prompt application of other colors. Thus, intuitive painting is a continual process of mistakes and corrections. Yet the correction of the mistake is so immediate that one may consider it a single process.

The student may not think or express his thoughts intuitively. Because of this he finds it difficult to conceive and execute an idea singly and completely. This second technique is a step toward the understanding and execution of the intuitive process through the medium of tempera paint—gaining a knowledge of color through experimentation in relation to an idea.

The third approach may be considered a decorative type of painting; that is, textures are applied to surfaces already dry. For example, an area of grass is first painted a dark-green color, and over it is laid fine streaks of light green. Thus, the dry-brush technique may give an impressionistic effect. The technique may also be used to indicate a three-dimensional quality. It further lends itself well to shadowed areas and perspective qualities.

However, the dry-brush technique must never be used as a substitute for learning. For example, if the effect of the dry-brush work is not preconceived as an integral part of the whole, it may be deemed an afterthought, in which case its result is due to a lack of knowledge or an act of laziness. As was stated in the opening chapter on painting, the student frequently applies "texture" in an attempt to reflect the nature of the "living" material. Such an attempt must be discouraged until the student realizes the nature of the things he is portraying. Otherwise, the expression becomes a falsehood. The student must at all times be honest with himself and realize mistakes in order to overcome them.

129

TOUCHDOWN. *This carefully conceived idea was also carefully painted.*

BOAT OVERTURNED. *Although this composition is complex and detailed, flexibility in technique adds excitement in color.*

Three approaches to the medium of tempera painting have been described briefly. There are undoubtedly others in which combinations of the approaches discussed above are involved. Not discussed at all is the technique related to an idea emotionally; that is, the technique used to strengthen, deepen, or accent an idea. This will be discussed in the chapter on motivation.

Evaluation

Again we must note the importance of evaluating the entire expression, and not merely the technique by which the expression evolves. Tempera painting may be judged by either one of the three approaches or none. In fact, the technique must never overshadow the idea being expressed; instead it must act as a harmonious ingredient that strengthens the idea. The expression must be witnessed and evaluated as a union of all necessary elements, and the major force of the painting must leave no doubt in the student's mind that factors supporting the whole are secondary.

The painting must be consistent in its technical application. A watercolor technique described as the first approach accompanied by an opaque application would hamper the consistency and unity of the whole. And there is no need for such inconsistencies to exist. A sky area, for example, need not be "airy" in the sense of light application of paint. The paint can still be applied heavily, but with light colors. Nor would it be wise to include the dry-brush technique with the process of mixing paint directly upon the paper. It would reveal not only a lack of personal organization, but a lack of knowledge as well. All compositional elements must be attracted to a focal point. Technical differences result in distraction and eventual destruction.

Finally, and most important, there is the appropriateness of the technique to the subject matter. Does the particular technique adapt itself to the object? This can only be answered in relation to the individual student. The art teacher should realize the potentialities of the student and the means by which his expression can best be projected.

TEMPTATION. *Appetizers were used to concoct this idea; the painted background unites the composition.*

132

Montage and Tempera Painting

An art form that is becoming more popular is the montage. Combined with tempera paint it affords an extensively creative experience and enables the student to intellectually and emotionally depict an experience coincidental with his personality.

The emotional and intellectual qualities can be reflected in the choice of subject matter and in the choice and application of paint. Because subject matter is already present in the form of magazine illustrations, photographs, and advertisements, it becomes a matter of selection. If the student has preconceived ideas, subject matter is then selected by identification with the ideas. Otherwise, the choice of subject matter dictates the type of expression to follow.

It may seem strange to use ideas already conceived and completed commercially. Yet, one does not actually use them. They merely act as a stimulus, for once the act of selection is complete, destruction of of those same ideas begins. The major compositional purpose of the montage is to destroy the ideas selected from magazine illustrations and photographs and, by retaining favored pieces, begin to rebuild an art form related to one's personality.

The choice of material may well indicate the attitudes, interests, and experiences of the student. After cutting numerous ideas from magazines, the student assimilates his material. He begins to destroy commercial compositions already complete. For example, an individual head has been clipped from the magazine page, and from the head is clipped the mouth. In turn, a mouth cut from another head is substituted in its place. A realistic portrayal is now transformed into one of unreality or surrealism.

The success of this substitution depends upon exact cutting and placement so that the transformation reveals a natural setting or surrounding. At the same time, consideration must be given to the type of

HAVE SOME FRUIT. *Success in this montage depended on the complete unification of paint and cut advertisements.*

LIFE. *The student utilized many of life's leisure pleasures for this complex design.*

HALL OF HORRORS. *This unusual pattern and the imaginative symbols create a typical science-fiction illustration.*

substitution. It is not enough to simply trade places. The transition must reflect an element of emotion or intellect. In other words, there must be a complete transformation from the original composition to the substitution in relation to emotional or intellectual transference. A head may be made comical, intriguing, ridiculous, or mysterious. And to extend this process further, one now attaches the head to a body that also has been transformed from the original composition.

Thus far, only single compositions have been considered. As the montage becomes more complex with the arrangement of new ideas, the application of paint becomes a factor in bringing the expression to its finality. Inconsistencies can destroy the montage before it reaches a climax in the manner in which paint is applied. Three factors govern the success of the expression: the technical application of paint, the choice of colors, and the arrangement of colors. All three factors must coincide with the choice of subject matter in relation to color and personality and in the placement of the subject matter.

In applying the paint, the student may choose to paint the background before pasting the ideas secured from magazines. In this manner he matches the ideas to the painted background. This order of attack may make the selection of ideas more difficult, but by this method the

135

MOMENT OF DECISION. *A former president was used as a symbol of a noble life in contrast to a life of pleasure; this shows an excellent use of tempera paint for background unity.*

psychological stage is set. The student then matches his ideas to the color, arrangement, and brushstroke of the paint.

One of the advantages of this procedure is that even though the background has been established, it remains feasible to change it to suit ideas that do not completely coincide with the color or brushstroke of the paint. Consequently, ideas may fluctuate in importance and in position depending on the difficulty in selecting material and also on the changing personality of the student.

If, however, the ideas are permanently placed, certain disadvantages come into play when the paint is applied. Frequently, the direction or movement of the paint when applied causes a change in ideas by deemphasis or overemphasis; that is, the brushstrokes call attention to themselves instead of strengthening the ideas by playing down the background. If this procedure is evidenced consistently throughout the expression, the original concept will be destroyed. Furthermore, the direction in which the brush moves frequently results in outlines caused by painting around the objects or ideas. This does not strengthen the presence of the object. Of course, the same procedure may be used purposefully to weaken particular ideas. In either case, the student must be fully aware of the potential results so that changes occur according to his desires and predictions.

Little has been said of the placement of objects or figures in relation to each other. Should figures overlap, or should they merely suggest overlapping? Can overlapping overplay its role? How does one suggest contact? These questions can be answered only in light of one's own knowledge. If overlapping acts as a strengthening element, then it should be used. Whatever approach is used, the result should indicate a connection of one idea to another so that isolated areas are nonexistent. However, crowded conditions result if objects simply overlap each other with no regard to interpenetration; that is, the placing of one object over another may destroy the original idea so that little meaning is left.

Perhaps an illustration will clarify this point: the student has cut out and pasted a figure of a man onto a painted background. He cuts off the head, and in its place pastes the head of a monkey. Now he substitutes the leg of a horse for the human leg. Furthermore, he places a large dinosaur foot over the human foot. And so in looking at the newly created figure, we find that the three changes made destroyed the original figure and that a fantastic creature resulted. In addition to these three changes a fourth

MEMORY. *Time pieces were used here as symbols of passing childhood; the application of paint can "make or break" a design.*

change is made, that of putting a huge cigarette advertisement into the mouth of the monkey head, thus completely obliterating the three newly created areas and destroying the major idea. Thus overlapping is overplayed.

This same overplay can be attributed to painting as well, or to the combination of montage and painting.

The montage painting is truly a painting experience if one so uses the montage technique in relation to painting that it acts only as an aid in producing ideas in graphic form.

Evaluation

Evaluation is based entirely upon the relationship of the montage to the painting; that is, the one enhances the other, but since the experience is considered to be a painting one, the technique of montage must always be subservient. In judging a montage painting one must consider the final outcome in terms of initial ideas. Granted that ideas may change as the student seeks to match his changing personality, frequently one's anxiety causes the expression "to go too far," and the ideas originally displayed are then no longer an important part of the composition. Such a change is valid if stronger ideas come into existence. If they do not, the montage painting weakens as it progresses, and eventually disorganization results.

Aside from the emotional, intellectual, and imaginative qualities that are always important in evaluating an art form, one must consider the naturalness of the expression. In spite of the destruction of complete compositions and the reconstruction of compositions of a fantastic nature, it is essential that the montage painting reveal an organization that is "unreal" but appears "natural." This paradox is managed by mechanical means, simply by cutting out exactly those illustrations to be used and then pasting them exactly in the positions they are to occupy. Herein, incidentally, lies the evaluative factor—the mechanical exactitude with which these objects or figures are transferred from the magazines to the montage painting.

Although this experience offers itself to the role of comedy, it is not at all impossible to include the serious side, as evidenced in some of the accompanying illustrations.

News. *This simple design used types of cloth and newspaper.*

140

Collage and Tempera Painting

The collage has for many years been considered an art form in itself. This is as it should be. Yet, one must go further than the execution as an art form complete in itself. It must be a motivation for future production in the form of painting. That is why the medium of paint is utilized in conjunction with the textural materials necessary for the construction of a collage.

The artist has used the collage type of expression in seeking new ways of self-expression and communication. The collage has always been considered a form of painting. Now, however, a different form of expression is considered in which attention is focused upon gathering and arranging natural materials. The application of paint is incidental or an excuse for lack of ingenuity in adapting a material to a given area.

Thus, the collage and tempera painting forwards three definite purposes. First, it awakens the student's awareness of nature by seeking and discovering individual differences in natural plant and animal life as well as the textural differences that exist in man-made products. Second, it integrates these natural objects with the medium of tempera paint so that the union of the two appears "natural." Third, it acts as a stimulus for future production in the area of painting in the application of the knowledge acquired to indicate or suggest textured areas.

Each of these three purposes demands investigation. Discovering natural textural material in our environment should stimulate and challenge the student. Thus, motivation in the expression of an idea is the first step. The student may first "draw an idea" and then conceive materials to be placed in the different sections of the depicted idea, or he may first decide upon certain materials to be used and then plan his idea to suit the materials. In either case, uncommon materials rather than the usual should be sought.

Some of the materials that are commonly collected for collage purposes and frequently result in a stereotype are dirt to be used as a ground surface, grass to be used as such, pebbles to be used as a road, cotton for clouds, pine needles for trees, paddle popsticks for telephone poles, toothpicks for fence posts, and buttons for eyes. Some of the uncommon materials to be used may be pieces of slate for a rooftop, black silt for smoke, kernels of corn for a stone walk, cut pieces of asphalt for the sides of buildings, and eggshells for stone walls.

The success of the collage tempera painting depends upon textural materials to which one responds both tactually and visually. A material must not only feel soft but also look soft. If it looks rough, it must also feel rough.

After the accumulation and permanent placement of these materials, tempera paint is added to unify the appearance of the composition. It is not unnatural for exuberance to supersede the integration of material and paint. The student becomes obsessed with the natural objects, so that the application of paint is generally nonexistent. Or paint is used only if the desired materials are unavailable. Rather than subordinate, the tempera paint should now become as significant as the textured material itself.

Let us consider a simple composition involving a tree and house on the ground with clouds in the sky above. Furthermore, let us assume that the tree was made up of the natural substance of bark and that the adjacent area of ground was painted a sandy color. There must be not only a contrast in texture between these two areas but a contrast in color as well. But the contrast in color should be at a minimum so that texture remains dominant. Also, the sky painted gray would act effectively to reduce color contrast throughout the expression.

Another effective use of color is its application to the material itself, which aids in toning down the sharp contrast between the color of the material and the color of the painted area. Tactual contrast is still evident, but the color contrast should be such as to present, in appearance, a tempera painting.

The third proposal leads to future production. The knowledge gained through purposeful visual perception of nature by the accumulation of natural objects and their application to an idea establishes the initial move toward the production of painting that is tactual in touch and in appearance.

142

LOCOMOTIVE. *This pictorial composition utilized descriptive objects; materials were painted to blend with the painted background.*

The adolescent has become involved in a visual world. Thus, he expresses things as visual representations rather than emotional reactions. The actual experience of touching the materials used in the collage aids in understanding the importance of textures found throughout his environment. The appearance of an old oak tree swinging nakedly high on a hill can be expressed more dramatically if the student is allowed to touch the bark of the tree and rub his fingers over its roughness. The roughness of the tree is visually apparent to the student, but that same roughness becomes real through physical contact. One may react emotionally to something that is seen but the greater the number of senses that participate in the reaction the more emotionally charged the subject becomes.

BIG CITY. *Enamel, dirt, and salt were used here to texturize the buildings; the paint quality is excellent.*

However, one must realize that the student has not yet learned to adapt this knowledge simultaneously with emotion. Knowledge of textures is intellectual, and when the intellect and emotion are evident in a painting, each must be controlled to further deepen and strengthen the subject being expressed. An illustration may clarify this point.

Swampland, seen for the first time by the student, may evoke reactions of distaste, indifference, or attraction. One must realize that these reactions stem from intellectual or emotional qualities. If the student reacts emotionally to the swamp scene, knowledge of the textural makeup will set up a more controlled balance between intellect and emotion. It is possible, of course, that even a closer view or study of the plant and animal life of the swamp area will do nothing to further the expression intellectually. Perhaps this is well, for when one is emotionally attracted to nature and is able to express that emotion, the intellect is of little matter. This is especially true of the student who needs not intellectual encouragement, but emotional stimulation to parallel the evident turn toward the visual and academic aspects of nature.

Intellectual pursuit is indeed essential, but if its introduction results in the elimination of emotional content, a potential artistic expression will never reach its goal.

One may now question the validity of the collage type of painting, since it seems to be a direct invitation to stimulate intellectual thinking. It is more than an invitation. It is a demand. Art is not emotion alone. Nor is it the intellect operating by itself. Emotions that take form in a painting must be controlled, and intellect is the rein by which the emotional expression is checked.

One hopes that the use of the collage approach to painting will eventually result in an intuitive approach to painting. The acquisition of textural knowledge must be integrated with one's emotions at the precise time that they are expressed through the medium of paint. One may react emotionally at the sight of a newborn baby's smooth skin. But to feel the softness of the skin will help in expressing the true nature of the skin. It is this knowledge gained through the visual and tactual senses that deepens the emotional response.

Evaluation

Evaluation of the collage type of painting depends upon the selection of materials (rarity, variety of textures) placement of materials, appropriate application of materials to an idea, balance of tempera paint to material, emotional qualities, and, finally, the overlap and interweave of paint and texture.

Since the basic purpose of the collage is to learn about one's environment, these basic materials should never lose their identity when applied with the paint, even though one of the evaluative factors is the interweave of paint and material. Each applied texture should enhance the area it serves and also adjacent areas that are in contrast to it. Furthermore, paint applied over a texture must not destroy the appearance or the tactual quality of the texture.

As stated earlier, the excitement of gathering materials may cause a loss of compositional awareness. Especially if the experience is a new one, the purpose of seeking materials and applying them to a flat surface may be lost to an overzealous drive. The student may find himself completing the activity in record time and thus losing much of the prescribed value. Initial enthusiasm must be tempered in the early stages so that the fullest benefit can be derived from the purposes set forth.

Another purpose of the collage is to promote future production in the light of the knowledge acquired, but it would, of course, be difficult to evaluate the collage itself by things yet to come. Frequently, however, there is an indication of the future that, in a sense, dictates the course the teacher must follow: that of complete evaluation. One must evaluate a prescribed assignment, but one must also evaluate the growth; so that some evaluations are not definite until other, follow-up experiences take place.

Therefore, the collage painting is evaluated as an expression in itself, but a complete evaluation must be withheld until evidence of textural application is found in future paintings.

146

SUGGESTED ACTIVITIES

Tempera Painting

1. Paint a landscape of early evening, stressing shadows.
2. Paint a rainy pavement.
3. Paint a seascape to stress the movement of water.
4. Paint a scene of rooftops with thawing snow.
5. Paint different scenes of sky. (cloudy, stormy, clear, foggy).
6. Paint a figure (woman) using only three cool colors.
7. Paint the same figure using three warm colors.
8. Paint a landscape by applying colors impressionistically side by side.
9. Paint a still life in a purposeful flat pattern.
10. Paint with a palette knife a scene of old buildings; scrape off or scratch in the paint to "age" the buildings.

Montage and Tempera Painting

Choose from magazines pictures that suggest one of the following themes:

1. Heads
2. Men and women
3. Adults and animals
4. Fashionable hair styles

5. Fantasy

6. Frivolity

7. Loneliness

8. Transportation

9. Athletics

10. Houses and people

Collage and Tempera Painting

Using *natural* materials, paste and paint ideas resembling the following:

1. House in the country

2. Downtown buildings

3. The farm

4. Seacoast

5. Trees and flowers in the country

Using artificial or substitute materials, paste and paint ideas resembling the following:

6. Mother and child

7. Animals on the farm

8. Abstract moods (joy, anger, love, peace)

9. Heads

10. Dinner table

148

FIGURE PAINTING WITH TEMPERA

14

Figure painting in tempera might well be included in the chapter on tempera painting except for one major difference. This chapter concerns tempera painting in a direct approach that focuses attention upon a given subject (still life setup; posed figures). Furthermore, efforts are not related to the projection or extension of ideas except as a climactic attempt to bring the expression to a conclusion. The direct approach to figure painting concerns itself with ideas only within the realm of the representation before the student; that is, the position, attitude, and character, or perhaps even costume, of the visual stimuli will determine emotionally or intellectually the ideas to be expressed. If a background is expressed in the painting, it is only to complete the expressed idea initiated by the natural stimuli. Ideas related to the process of tempera paintings are discussed in Chapter 13.

Since ideas are not necessarily involved, they do not dictate the colors to be used. Color is already present in the makeup of the stimuli, namely, the still life setup or the posed model. However, this is not to say that the emotional quality or the personality of the stimulus, as well as the emotional or intellectual reaction one has toward the stimulus itself, should not be evidenced in the expression. But the problem of painting is simplified by the elimination of ideas, and since color is the predominant factor in the success of this experience, the student is relieved of the initial barrier to creative expression. Communication and expression will be evident in the painting in a subjective manner, which can be arrived at more naturally and readily.

By direct approach to painting, preconceived concepts and pre-planning are eliminated. Generally, painting is preceded by a "feeling out" process in which the student draws in pencil, crayon, or chalk the image before him. Paint is then mixed on a palette to ensure that the color to be applied is appropriate to the material. This affords reflection on both the colors to be used and the ideas to be expressed.

STUDY OF GIRL'S HEAD. *This was painted directly from a model; the time was limited to retain a suggestive quality.*

However, our concern in the direct approach is somewhat similar to that of contour drawing in which the eye and hand work coordinately; that is, the student paints directly while looking at the model. Naturally, because color is involved, the process is more difficult. The blending of color is executed directly on the paper, which for the uninformed student causes immediate frustration. The results of the color blend are indefinite and unidentifiable. If the student desires a flesh tone for the face, he must first realize the colors that constitute a flesh color. Let us assume that the three colors, red, yellow, and white are to be used. The

150

GIRL ON ROCK. *This was a quick pencil sketch with the background added; the colors were blended directly on the paper to retain excitement.*

student must know the ratio of each color. If he first applies red, then white may be applied and result in a pink color. Yellow is then added to give the face a flesh tone. With considerable practice one learns to stagger these colors in the degree they are to be used. However, it would be expedient to first apply the lightest color, white, then add yellow slowly, and finally red. Furthermore, the paper on which these colors are applied must always be kept wet to a degree that the paints can be moved about. If the paint should dry, another added color would not blend, so that the process would begin anew.

WAITING. *This was painted directly from a model; the background was changed to suit the particular idea.*

If layers of paint accumulate, eventual cracking will result, in which case the entire expression must be reinitiated.

Let us examine closer what happens as the paint is applied. The student first applies white to the areas that are least recessive in order to establish light and dark areas. Yellow and red are then added to form the flesh tone. The process of mixing these three colors directly on the paper will eventually be carried on with speed and accuracy; but more important, an intuitive expression may emerge. Thus, after repeated "failures," the student will master the fundamentals of color blending

152

HAT SHOPPE AT EASTER. *The seated pose of this model correlates with the idea; the colors are typical of Easter Sunday; the white cross in the background symbolizes the hope of Christians.*

and color relationship and apply that knowledge simultaneously with ideas.

If this direct application of paint is not demanded of students, many will fall to dictation of the primary lines expressed to represent the figure. Once a line is drawn to indicate a direction, shape, or form, the student finds himself painting within the confines he has set for himself. As much as he attempts to extend beyond those boundaries, he generally succumbs to a routine pattern of self-confinement, thus damaging his imaginative and emotional powers.

GIRL WITH FLOWER. *Here the introduction of the background was a deliberate contrast to the rigid pose of the model.*

Another advantage of this approach is the eventual elimination of the outline. The use of the outline in this proposal is completely forbidden. Use of it would defeat the very purpose of the approach; for not only is the knowledge of color one of its aims, but just as important is the elimination of stereotype productions to which the outline is a contributing factor. Furthermore, the outline would destroy the three-dimensional quality that is so essential in this type of painting.

154

FIGURE AT THE WINDOW. *This is an intuitive response to a posed model; the window was added to coincide with other rectangular shapes.*

As the student proceeds to paint the remainder of the "body," he must realize the continuity of the whole so that the final expression is not a segmented composition. Frequently, the student will exhaust himself in mastering the color application of the face, which is generally the most important feature. Completing the composition is a trial until he visualizes the whole. As he paints one area, he must think of the areas yet to be painted. But if he concerns himself with the whole too soon or

155

GIRL AND PINE TREES. *This wet paper approach reveals subtlety and charm; much can be done with a few brush strokes.*

156

APARTMENT HOUSE. *This is a strong monumental painting of a simple pose; it was quickly painted; details were merely suggested.*

before he masters the color blend, the component parts will not unify because there is a lack of three-dimensional qualities and also because there is an indefinite contrast relationship.

Another interesting result is the speeding-up process once the essential feature of the face is complete. Less importance is attached to the body, and consequently the painting is completed hurriedly and without thought. This entire approach demands practice and concentration so that in its finality it reveals an emotional and intuitive reaction to the natural stimulus. Furthermore, it enables the student to express his ideas confidently and with a heightened interest and challenge.

157

MAN ON A STUMP. *The strong application of paint here reflects the personality of the student; the background technique is consistent with the painted figure.*

VISITATION DAY. *Here single-posed figures were arranged in groups on surfaces; this was painted with palette knives.*

YOUNG COUPLE. *This shows rather crude drawing but has a stimulating paint quality; the idea was developed from posed models.*

160

Evaluation

Evaluation is based first upon the knowledge of color, second, on the emotional quality, and third, on the development of the background area.

To evaluate the knowledge of color, one must realize the particular style or technique at which the student finally arrives. It may be impressionistic in nature, realistic, naturalistic, or expressionistic, but in all instances it must reveal a high degree of knowledge of color blend and a confident brushstroke.

A second evaluative factor is emotion. Difficult as it is to define emotion, the sensitive art educator should quite readily evaluate emotional qualities. An expression reflects either joy, pleasure, love, loneliness, anger, warmth, sociability, comedy, drama, or satire. One must admit that the student frequently reveals emotions within his expression but is unaware that they exist. The educator is apt to evaluate the expression on the same basis; that is, a misplacement or misinterpretation of emotion may lead to a false evaluation.

Development of an appropriate background indicates imaginative powers since its expression stems from ideas not necessarily attributed to the natural stimulus of the posed figure. Furthermore, color must coincide with the visual stimulus as well as the emotion connected with it.

Above all, one must judge subjectively; that is to say, color relationship and techniques must be considered in the sense that they serve or strengthen an idea emotionally.

161

SUGGESTED ACTIVITIES

Suggested themes to be expressed. Student or professional models are to be used whenever possible, and the painting is to be completed with a background adjusted to the poses.

1. Having my picture taken
2. Perched on a tree stump in the country
3. Watching a parade
4. Lying on the beach
5. The rodeo
6. Standing in the lunch line
7. Looking out of my window
8. Waiting on tables in a restaurant
9. Window shopping
10. Walking to school

MOTIVATION OF IDEAS   15

Seasonal Themes

In dealing with seasonal themes one must be alert to pitfalls of artistic sacrifice. It is a simple matter to succumb to historical data, stereotype symbols, and shallow ideas. When the question arises, "But what did they look like in those days," the art teacher must realize that the question is of a serious nature and cannot be answered insincerely or callously. The question indicates an interest in the history of the times. But the teacher must question the purpose of this interest. If it is to satisfy the assignment, which presumably would result in a nonartistic portrayal, one must then question the validity of the interest. Moreover, if the interest is to strengthen one's knowledge of history for its own sake, it serves no purpose in the art world.

Even if the purpose in seeking an answer to this question were to deepen the spirit of art through a greater knowledge of historical fact, one might then question the time element in uncovering such facts. For if one answer is sought, undoubtedly other questions will follow, such as, "Did they wear their hair long?" "Did they wear beards?" "What color was their skin?" Such questions must lead to periods of research requiring time that will not further the desire to depict ideas of a seasonal nature. If such research must be established, then let it be in the area of the social sciences.

The business of stereotype symbols will always be a major problem of the art educator, but with dedication of purpose and a greater knowledge of the avenues that art now travels, along with a sensitivity of control, it may be minimized. Stereotype symbols such as Santa Claus, fireplaces with the routine Christmas stockings, stylized carolers, the old fashioned sleigh, and the small church in the wilderness are increasingly evident in the seasonal theme of Christmas. How, then, does one begin to combat such stereotype symbols and foster the ideas that make it unnecessary to express repeated patterns of thought? Secondly, how does

HALLOWEEN BALL. *Here posed models were altered to suit the idea; this has an interesting division of black and white areas.*

CHRISTMAS VACATION. *Again, posed models were used to substantiate gestures; this was painted quite freely to retain the excitement of winter sports.*

one attack the inability to express significant ideas in a purposeful and subjective manner—the ideas are evident but the presentation is stylized?

In the first instance, the art teacher must permit the student less time to think about ideas pertinent to the theme. Instead, visual stimuli must be the source of future production. Through mutual agreement, posed models may depict a theme. Since the models act as the stimulus, the student need not reflect on ideas that he has repeatedly expressed. Thus, his attention is focused upon given figures; namely, the models. The idea is there before him as a constant reminder of his duty. Truly a

165

LENTEN SEASON. *This gesture painting of the crucifixion theme was done in the passionate colors of purple and black.*

challenge has been set before him, and undoubtedly discouragement accompanies his every move. But confidence is never gained through backtracking.

The same stimulus can be used to erase the stylization expressed by the student. Using the theme of Christmas carolers as an example, the teacher now poses students to act as carolers. The problem here is not one of stimulating ideas but of motivating the manner in which the idea is to be expressed. Before proceeding further, it is necessary to clarify the

166

CHRISTMAS EVE. *Here the spirit of Christmas was focused on the humble and poverty stricken.*

word "stylization." To many, the word "style" means success. The development of a style is the trademark of successful entertainers. One may sing in the style of Bing Crosby, speak in the style of Richard Burton, dance in the style of Fred Astaire, play golf in the style of Jack Nicklaus, or paint in the style of John Marin. The style of each of these successes reflects his own personality, yet each is mature and has materialized after years of concentration and frustration. Each style is appropriate to the person using it.

167

SINGING THE PSALMS. *These subdued colors present a theme of mourning—before the glorious day to follow.*

If the student's style indicates strength and potential, it would be unwise to change it. However, if the style hinges on superficiality, a direct approach is necessary to lead the student to an entirely new outlook. Therefore, the style of which we speak is unfounded because it stems from unreality. For example, using the idea of the carolers, the figures are expressed with a definite lack of spirit. If the spirit of Christmas is being expressed through the medium of caroling, then there must be evidence of it. Instead, we find rosy-cheeked faces with open mouths, turned-up noses, and elongated eyelashes. Students who use this type of portrayal are depicting not the spirit of an idea, but a sterile repetition of earlier growth.

It is now necessary to indicate these faults to the student. One can do so by presenting reality in the form of posed models in the act of

168

HALLOWEEN PARTY. *Spooky masks and a strong paint quality present this emotional expression.*

singing Christmas carols. The procedure is not new, but it has been sidelined by teachers who feel that the enforcement hampers the creative thought process because it stems from reality and from reality comes distortion and exaggeration. Furthermore, teachers have felt that inhibitions multiply when students are confronted with figure drawing because of their inability to draw the human form. But if the student is not challenged in this regard, he is continually frustrated because he deeply desires to master the problem. As the carolers sing the spirit of Christmas, the teacher indicates the points of interest. The mouth, as it sings different words, changes the formation of the face. A widely opened mouth will elongate the chin and foreshorten the nose. And in order for one to understand these changes, one must first understand the structure of the human face.

Gestures evidence themselves also in the figure, as in the arms and hands. These gestures suggest the spirit of Christmas visually just as the singing voices suggest the spirit aurically. The clothing also indicates the movement of the body by the presence of the folds and creases. The texture of the clothing material indicates the intensity or subtlety of the spirit. These visual aspects of the idea of the Christmas carolers will assist in the understanding of the spirit of singing carols as well as furthering the knowledge of the human form.

Perhaps the most important and controversial aspect of the expression of seasonal themes is the actual meaning being conveyed. Really, this should be no problem at all. Yet it is. Religious intolerance is still widely prevalent. This is a shame, because it has deprived countless children of the right to express their personal loves and desires. One may question the relationship of religion to a seasonal theme. Such questioning has been the partial cause of the ever-increasing use of shallow ideas. The seasonal themes mentioned in this chapter directly or indirectly stem from religious sources. Christmas, Easter, New Year's Day, Halloween, Thanksgiving, Memorial Day, and Fourth of July are some of the important holidays that the American people celebrate and that the student commemorates through the art experience.

Stimulating creative thought through spiritual channels is indeed a difficult task. Let us consider the theme of Christmas, since we have already covered some of its aspects. Before any art experience can materialize, the proper atmosphere must be staged. A brief informal discussion of the major interpretations of the theme must be initiated, and during the discussion, the important ideas should be charted. Questions like the following may be projected. "What does Christmas mean to you?" "Why does the Christian world celebrate Christmas?" "Whose birthday was it?" "How has the birth of this person affected your life?" "What is the purpose of giving?" "Do you receive gifts on your birthday?"

Questions of this nature, if informally and tactfully presented, will open the "doors of thought" for many who never relate the birth of Christ to their own birth. The mother-and-child theme will have a deeper and more intimate meaning if focused upon the twentieth century. Historical facts clog the imagination, and to relate Christmas as it was centuries ago dims the personal experience necessary for the creation of art. Once these ideas are formulated, stimulation toward the manner of expression is established. Visual stimuli representing these ideas take the form of models, who can be shifted in pose to correspond to individual ideas.

For example, the mother-and-child theme can easily be portrayed because of its simplicity. A student posing as the mother pretends to hold the baby. Students acting as shepherds may be kneeling, strongly suggesting present-day humility; the gesture of giving may be represented by the outstretched arms of the posed students. Informal groupings may be included to satisfy the more advanced students if they desire more difficult poses. Emerging from this serious atmosphere will be an informal flexible situation initiated by a firm direct approach.

The use of informal questioning, the minimizing of historical data, the relationship of the event to the twentieth century, the use of familiar backgrounds and the use of visual stimuli are some of the means by which a greater and deeper meaning can be gained in the expression of seasonal themes.

GOOD FRIDAY. *Here the crucifixion theme was painted in swirling and dynamic colors; literal representation was practically eliminated.*

172

ALMSGIVING. *The simplicity of the idea and the composition makes this a strong painting.*

MOSES AND THE TEN COMMANDMENTS. *An expressive paint quality makes this a tremendously powerful expression.*

174

Moral and Spiritual Values

We speak of moral and spiritual values as factors necessary for the development of the individual. We know that history has recorded the need for spiritual aid in the solution of our greatest problems, for there can be little existence of an individual unless he possesses, or is in search of, truth; only then will his life be greatly strengthened. Tolerance, humility, integrity, and consistency are good educational qualities that should be explored and transplanted into the makeup of children.

The success of such a transformation is logically planted as the seed of creative expression. Art by its very nature is spiritual, and the art educator is duty bound to evoke the inner life of the student and project it into an outward expression. His heart and mind should be guided beyond personal satisfaction and embrace all of humanity. Personal gratification is perhaps foremost, and encouragement of this effect should be stimulated. However, students frequently fall into a pit of stagnancy or superiority unless their minds and hearts are led to a more satisfying state: the state of bringing joy and beauty to others.

This is a difficult task, especially in relation to spiritual and moral application. It presents a number of problems, foremost among them being the possibility of relinquishing any artistic expression the individual may project. There has always been the need to determine which is of paramount importance: the artistic child or the socially acceptable one. It is a tremendous task for the art educator to retain artistic creativity in the process of manipulating the inner and outer worlds of the individual.

The troubled, frustrated, neurotic student, once he is induced to express his emotional world, generally produces uninhibited and artistic expressions that frequently are lost when he is socially accepted. We believe we must educate through art. Thus, the production of the socially adjusted individual is foremost. Art is a means to this end, but art must also strive to retain creative expression at its fullest throughout

BEHIND THE DOOR. *An unfortunate victim of circumstance is shown being given assistance; a limited color palette helped.*

the life of the individual. Art serves a very vital area in molding the emotional life that transpires under the increased instinctive drives that lie unliberated during earlier childhood.

In order to accomplish this molding, it is first necessary to identify right and wrong to establish an inner security with which to creatively express an idea. Further complications become evident when the student is confronted by social changes, disturbed family relationships, and economic insecurities. Creativity enables the student to define his experiences and to establish a settlement between opposing forces of right

176

HUNGARY UNDER HITLERISM. *A Hungarian student depicted scenes of shacklement in terror stricken Hungary.*

and wrong. Those of use who have wronged others, and recognize the wrong, know the pangs of shame. And through knowing, a transformation toward good is possible. This theme is not intended to emphasize wrong, but only to recognize it and initiate a movement toward good through creative expression.

A period of careful motivation must precede such an undertaking, and strong emphasis must be placed upon the seriousness of the task. In actuality, the problem lies in the attempt of the student to express man's abuse of nature, and to reveal a means of combating such abuses. For

POLIO VICTIM. *Here personal experience led the student to depict his own portrayal; a student posed for this expression.*

example, fire, in itself, is good. The misuse of it can be injurious to nature. Money, in itself, is good, but if used to gain power, it generates greed. Food is essentially good, but it may lead to gluttony. The teacher must ever be aware of the forces of right and wrong and the value of moral and spiritual application. Abstract words such as fire, hate, love, sympathy, and anger lend themselves to a challenge in a proposed attempt to express an emotional reaction to one of these abstract states. The effect upon our natural resources, or upon ourselves, that any one of these

178

AT THE SCENE OF AN ACCIDENT. *Posed models were used to portray this scene of a traffic accident; the figure in the center is a mother sorrowing over a lost loved one.*

words may have will appear quite remote unless we adapt or adjust them to actual experiences.

Since the primary purpose of the creative act is to release tensions and fears in order to adjust oneself to the normal ways of life, it follows that art must unselfishly serve all of humanity. Many students refuse to open their hearts and minds to ideas that are wrong. Shame continues toward frustration until that rebellious attitude takes the form of destruction. It may well be that students are unable to express wrong acts

179

FISHERMAN'S PRAYER. *Here the masts of a ship take the form of three crosses; this intuitively expressed painting reflects the turmoil of the sea, yet suggests the soft meditating voice of the fisherman.*

180

through immediate experiences, but most certainly indirect sources are available for more remote cases. It simply leads to an objective expression by those who are remotely concerned. A tragic accident causing the death of a boy's father is an immediate experience for the boy, and the expression of such an event may be a subjective release. The boy's classmates might well express the same incident. The results would be less subjective, but nevertheless an expression of awareness that such a tragedy might have been averted.

Artists throughout the centuries have painted the social scene: man's injustice to man. It would seem that the greatest significance art holds for society is the self-gratification, the emotional release, the sheer enjoyment and relaxation, and the spiritual uplift for those who possess the integrity to follow such a course.

The presentation of thoughts of this nature may take varied forms. A study of past historical events and the artistic attempts to portray such events and the study of contemporary artists and their concerns are two ways of projecting a background and a springboard for interest and motivation. It would seem that once the background has been established and motivation extended, the further approach would be a casual and informal one, yet quite personal. Using abstract words, the teacher may discuss thoughts that lead to personal and social adjustments.

"What are some of the destructive forces of fire?" "How has man become a part of such forces?" "What does the word *crash* suggest to you?" "How have jealousy and envy caused harm to our fellow man? Revenge?" Hatred among peoples has caused devastation throughout the world. How can we change our ways in rectifying these tragedies?" Questions of this nature, if presented informally and objectively, will lead to a creative atmosphere and a seriousness with which to probe deeper into the student's mental and spiritual makeup.

As mentioned earlier, the basic purpose involved here is the recognition of the abuses of man toward man and his environment. Once this is realized, it becomes a matter of expressing it artistically in an attempt to curb such abuses through moral and spiritual application. The paintings accompanying this chapter reveal, in some instances, only the recognition of the abuses of good. Others relate both the abuses of nature and the inevitable aid toward the solution of the problems. It is not a problem of inflicting wrong upon the student, but of consciously attempting to show the effects of wrong acts upon man.

The reader may ask, "But should students be confronted with the morally wrong aspects of nature? Why emphasize the wrongs of man? Why not accentuate the good?" This is not the problem at all. The author only wishes to make more evident the abuses of good; and since these traits stem from the student's own personal background and experience, it does not become a motivating force or an invitation to do wrong. These traits are already present within the individual, and only he has evidence of it.

Many expressions of the students may release fears and tensions. If this be so, then comes the further attempt to overcome these fears through hope. This may take time, but with the recognition of the problem, a reaction takes place, and inevitably, some good will result. Other expressions may reveal an objective approach: an "outsider's" view of society. Experiences may be limited, but the capacity for alertness to and awareness of the problems of others may result in a sympathetic form of expression. Within society there are many who are aware of the problems of their fellow man and display a wealth of sympathy, courage, and patience. Yet they remain outside the emotional reactions that take place within the suffering.

Ultimately, this is the goal: to extend sympathy and love toward those less fortunate people who have become victims of man's inhumanity, to recognize the good within us, and to exercise this good to the fullest, so that in its recognition and practice a better individual will result.

SUGGESTED ACTIVITIES

Seasonal Themes

Suggested themes to be discussed and expressed:

1. Christmas: Madonna and child
2. Christmas: Carolers
3. Thanksgiving: Prayer
4. Halloween: Costume ball
5. Pre-Lenten: Mardi Gras
6. Easter: Resurrection
7. Easter: Rebirth of plant life
8. Memorial Day: Parade
9. Labor Day: Political speeches
10. Yom Kippur: Passover

Moral and Spiritual Values

Suggested themes to be discussed and expressed:

1. Apartment house fire
2. Clown: Theme of sorrow and joy
3. The funeral
4. Loss of one's pet
5. Automobile accident
6. Floods: Effects upon the homeless
7. Drought: Effect upon the farmer
8. Doctor and patient
9. The unemployed
10. Poverty: Effect upon family

These activities should stem from visual stimuli as much as possible. The most practical source is a student model.

INDEX

185